Reading & Writing
Angkor Wat

NATIONAL GEOGRAPHIC
L E A R N I N G

Australia • Brazil • Mexico • Singapore • United Kingdom • United States

National Geographic Learning,
a Cengage Company

Reading & Writing, Angkor Wat

**Laurie Blass, Mari Vargo, Keith S. Folse,
April Muchmore-Vokoun, Elena Vestri**

Publisher: Sherrise Roehr

Executive Editor: Laura LeDréan

Managing Editor: Jennifer Monaghan

Digital Implementation Manager,
Irene Boixareu

Senior Media Researcher: Leila Hishmeh

Director of Global Marketing: Ian Martin

Regional Sales and National Account
Manager: Andrew O'Shea

Content Project Manager: Ruth Moore

Senior Designer: Lisa Trager

Manufacturing Planner: Mary Beth Hennebury

Composition: Lumina Datamatics

For permission to use material from this text or product,
submit all requests online at **cengage.com/permissions**
Further permissions questions can be emailed to
permissionrequest@cengage.com

Student Edition: Reading & Writing, Angkor Wat
ISBN-13: 978-0-357-13828-1

National Geographic Learning
20 Channel Center Street
Boston, MA 02210
USA

Locate your local office at **international.cengage.com/region**

Visit National Geographic Learning online at **ELTNGL.com**
Visit our corporate website at **www.cengage.com**

Printed in China
Print Number: 02   Print Year: 2019

PHOTO CREDITS

Scope and Sequence

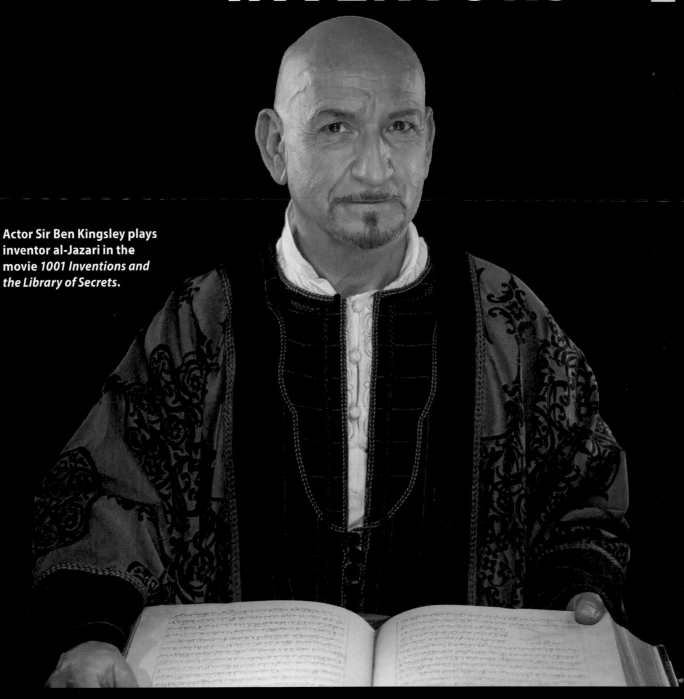

Actor Sir Ben Kingsley plays inventor al-Jazari in the movie *1001 Inventions and the Library of Secrets*.

ACADEMIC SKILLS

THINK AND DISCUSS

A **Look at the information on these pages and answer the questions.**

1. Who developed the first helicopter that flew with a pilot? When?
2. Who completed the first signal flare? When?
3. Who invented the first life raft? When?
4. Which invention do you think was most important? Why?

B **Use the correct form of the words in yellow to complete the definitions.**

If you _____ something, you give details about it.

If you _____ something, you are the first person to make it.

A _____ is an object that uses power to move.

A helicopter crew rescues a pilot floating in a life raft.

A WORLD OF INVENTIONS

Many people know that Thomas Edison **invented** the lightbulb. However, many inventors of other everyday items are not well known at all. Here are some examples of life-changing inventions with not-so-famous inventors.

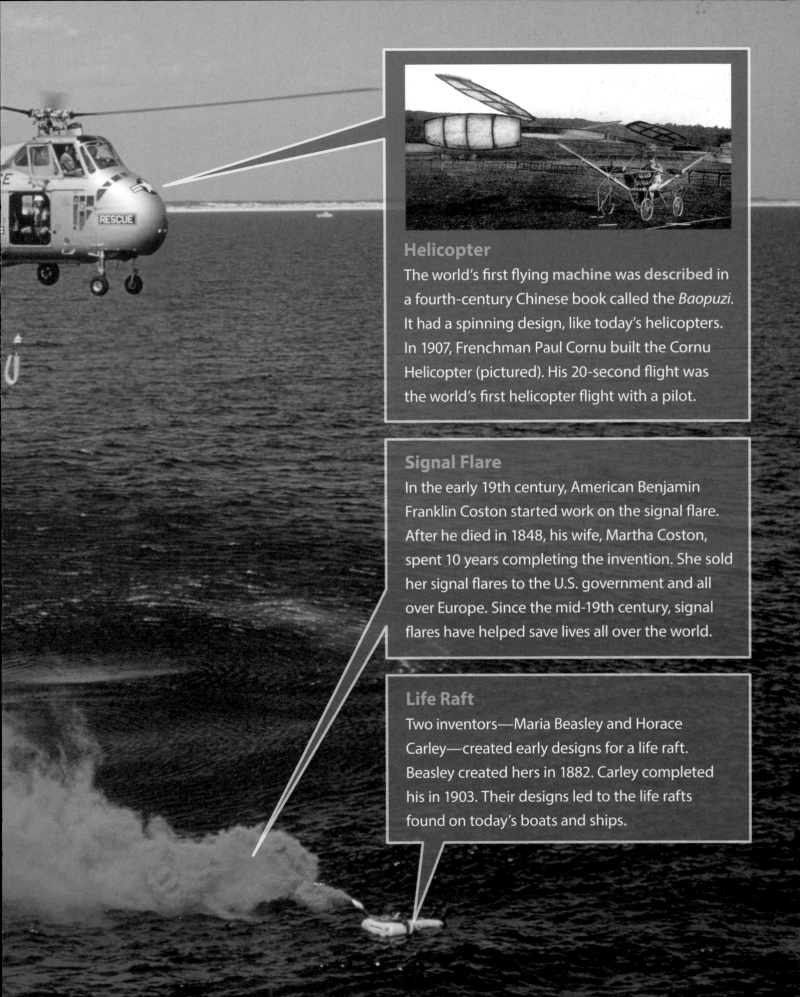

Helicopter

The world's first flying **machine** was **described** in a fourth-century Chinese book called the *Baopuzi*. It had a spinning design, like today's helicopters. In 1907, Frenchman Paul Cornu built the Cornu Helicopter (pictured). His 20-second flight was the world's first helicopter flight with a pilot.

Signal Flare

In the early 19th century, American Benjamin Franklin Coston started work on the signal flare. After he died in 1848, his wife, Martha Coston, spent 10 years completing the invention. She sold her signal flares to the U.S. government and all over Europe. Since the mid-19th century, signal flares have helped save lives all over the world.

Life Raft

Two inventors—Maria Beasley and Horace Carley—created early designs for a life raft. Beasley created hers in 1882. Carley completed his in 1903. Their designs led to the life rafts found on today's boats and ships.

Reading 1 QUICK READ SEE PAGE 110

PREPARING TO READ

BUILDING
VOCABULARY

A The words in **blue** below are used in the reading passage on pages 5–6. Match the sentence parts to make definitions. Use a dictionary to help you.

1. An **engine** _____
2. A **drawing** _____
3. **History** _____
4. A **model** _____
5. An **engineer** _____

a. works to build or fix things like machines, roads, or bridges.
b. is the part of a machine that gives it power.
c. is an object that is a copy of something else.
d. refers to events that happened in the past.
e. is a picture of something made with a pen or pencil.

BUILDING
VOCABULARY

B Circle the correct word to complete the definitions.

1. If something **floats** in water, it **will / won't** stay on the top of the water.

2. If something **sinks** in water, it **will / won't** stay on the top of the water.

USING
VOCABULARY

C List three ideas for each category below. Then share your ideas with a partner.

1. three things that **float** in water

_____ _____ _____

2. three things that **sink** in water

_____ _____ _____

3. three things that have an **engine**

_____ _____ _____

4. three famous people from **history**

_____ _____ _____

PREDICTING

D Read the first paragraph of the reading passage on pages 5–6. What invention does it describe? Why does the author describe the invention as "amazing"? Note your ideas below. Then discuss with a partner.

_____

_____

THE FATHER OF ENGINEERING

🎧 Track 1

A. Eight hundred years ago, a man in southern Turkey invented an amazing clock. It was more than 23 feet (seven meters) high. At its base[1] was a life-size model elephant. Every half hour, something amazing happened. The whole clock came alive: Model birds, dragons,[2] and people started to move.

B. The clock's inventor was an engineer named al-Jazari. He lived in Diyarbakir, a city in Turkey. Al-Jazari was probably one of the greatest engineers in history. Some historians[3] call him "the father of modern-day engineering."

C. We know about al-Jazari mostly from a book that he wrote. It describes a number of machines of all shapes and sizes. They include clocks, hand-washing machines, and pumps[4] for lifting water. The book also has drawings that show how each machine works.

D. Many everyday items today—from toys to car engines—still use al-Jazari's ideas. Without his machines with moving parts, we might not have modern-day robots.

E. Today, it is still possible to see what al-Jazari's elephant clock looked like. A full-size working model is in Dubai's Ibn Battuta Mall. There, every half hour, al-Jazari's most amazing invention comes to life once again.

[1]The **base** of something is its bottom part.
[2]In stories, a **dragon** is a large animal that looks like a lizard with wings.
[3]A **historian** is a person who studies history.
[4]A **pump** is a machine that makes air or water move in a certain direction.

How Does the Elephant Clock Work?

A bowl with a small hole floats in a water tank inside the elephant's body ①. As the bowl slowly sinks, it pulls a rope that moves a human figure ②. His moving pen shows the number of minutes past the hour.

Every half hour, the water bowl becomes full and sinks completely. This causes a ball to fall from the top of the clock ③. The movement of the ball causes a phoenix to move and make a sound.

The ball then drops out of a falcon's mouth into the mouth of a Chinese dragon ④. The weight of the ball causes the dragon's head to move down ⑤, and the dragon's tail pulls the water bowl back up.

Finally, the ball drops out of the dragon's mouth and into a vase ⑥. As the ball lands in the vase, the elephant driver moves and makes a sound ⑦. The cycle[5] begins again until there are no more balls in the top of the clock.

[5] A **cycle** is a series of events that starts again after it has finished.

Phoenix

Falcon

Dragon

Pen

Vase

▶ **In his elephant clock, al-Jazari used ideas from Egypt, China, Greece, and India. The clock was therefore also a celebration of different cultures.**

UNDERSTANDING THE READING

A Complete the summary. Use no more than three words for each blank.

Al-Jazari was a(n) ¹ _____ who lived in ² _____
around ³ _____ ago. His most famous invention was the
⁴ _____. We know about al-Jazari and his ideas because he
⁵ _____. Many modern-day items or machines use al-Jazari's ideas,
such as a car ⁶ _____.

B How does al-Jazari's elephant clock work? Write the
steps (a–e) in the correct sequence in the diagram.

a. The dragon's tail pulls the bowl back up.
b. After 30 minutes, a ball starts to fall from
   the top.
c. A bowl floats on the water in the tank.
d. The bowl moves down in the water and pulls on ropes.
e. The ball drops into a dragon's mouth.

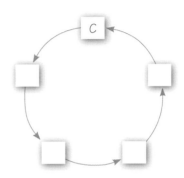

> **CRITICAL THINKING**   **Analyzing** an argument means looking at and
> understanding a writer's point of view. As you read, ask yourself: *What is the writer's
> opinion? What evidence does the writer give to support this opinion?*

C Note answers to the questions below. Then discuss with a partner.

1. In paragraph B, what opinion does the author give of al-Jazari?

   _____

2. What evidence does the author use to support his/her opinion?

   _____

◀ **A full-size working
model of the elephant
clock in Ibn Battuta Mall,
Dubai**

DEVELOPING READING SKILLS

READING SKILL Understanding Pronoun Reference

A pronoun is a word that stands for, or takes the place of, a noun. **Subject pronouns** are *I, he, she, it, you, we,* and *they*. Subject pronouns refer to subjects in sentences. A pronoun usually refers to a noun that comes earlier—in the same sentence or in a previous sentence.

To understand which noun a pronoun refers to, ask yourself these questions:

- Is the pronoun singular (e.g., *he, she, it*) or plural (e.g., *they*)? The pronoun should match the earlier noun.
- Is the pronoun feminine (*she*), masculine (*he*), or gender-neutral (*it, they*)? The gender of the pronoun should match the gender of an earlier noun.

In the example below, the singular masculine pronoun **he** refers to the man **al-Jazari**. The plural gender-neutral pronoun **they** refers to the plural noun **machines**.

*A man named **al-Jazari** was one of the greatest inventors in history. **He** invented amazing **machines**. **They** were both beautiful and useful.*

UNDERSTANDING
PRONOUNS

A Look at the **bold** pronouns in the paragraph below. Ask these questions about each pronoun:

- Is it singular or plural?
- Is it feminine, masculine, or gender-neutral?

We know about al-Jazari mostly from a book that **he** wrote. **It** describes a number of machines of all shapes and sizes. **They** include clocks, hand-washing machines, and pumps for lifting water. The book also has drawings that show how each machine works.

UNDERSTANDING
PRONOUNS

B In the paragraph above, draw an arrow to the noun that each pronoun refers to.

▶ **Pages from al-Jazari's *Book of Knowledge* show one of his water-raising machines.**

Sir Ben Kingsley as al-Jazari in the movie *1001 Inventions and the Library of Secrets*

THE GOLDEN AGE

BEFORE VIEWING

A Look at the title of the video. The phrase *Golden Age* is used to talk about times in history when people achieved great things. What period in your country's history could be described as a Golden Age? Discuss with a partner.

DISCUSSION

B The words below are used in the video. Match each word with the correct definition.

VOCABULARY IN CONTEXT

> The elephant clock was an **ingenious** invention.
> Al-Jazari's ideas helped lay the **foundations** of modern engineering.
> Al-Jazari's work has had a big **impact** on today's technology.
> Ancient Egypt is an example of a very old **civilization**.

1. _____ (n) a strong effect

2. _____ (n) the ideas that other things are based on

3. _____ (adj) new and very clever

4. _____ (n) a group of people with their own society and culture

C Read the information about the Dark Ages. Then answer the questions.

As the Roman Empire spread through Europe, it brought with it many improvements in art and culture. However, after the Roman Empire fell in around A.D. 500, many of these improvements were lost. This period, which lasted hundreds of years, became known as the Dark Ages. Modern historians, however, prefer not to use the term Dark Ages anymore. Research has shown that many great achievements were made in this period, both in Europe and in other parts of the world.

1. Why is the period after A.D. 500 known as the Dark Ages?

   _____

2. Why do some historians think that the name is not suitable?

   _____

WHILE VIEWING

A ▶ Watch the video. What are two reasons why the librarian believes the Dark Ages should be known as "the Golden Ages"?

☐ a. There were many great discoveries made during this time.

☐ b. Many great artists and writers were born during the period.

☐ c. Ideas from many different cultures around the world came together.

B ▶ Watch the video a second time. Match the sentence parts to make true sentences.

1. Ibn al-Haytham _____   a. made discoveries about engineering.

2. Abbas ibn Firnas _____   b. had early ideas about flying.

3. Al-Jazari _____   c. explained how our eyes work.

AFTER VIEWING

A What modern technology may have benefited from the work of the inventors below? Use information from the video and the reading passage on pages 5–6.

1. Ibn al-Haytham: _____

2. Abbas ibn Firnas: _____

3. Al-Jazari: _____

B Which of the people in activity **A** do you think made the most useful discoveries? Why? Discuss with a partner.

Reading 2

QUICK READ SEE PAGE 113

PREPARING TO READ

A The words in **blue** below are from the reading passage on pages 12–13. Match the correct form of each word to its definition.

BUILDING VOCABULARY

Bill Gates is sometimes called "the father of home computing." Born in 1955, Gates **grew up** in the United States. When he was 13, his school bought one of the earliest computers, and Gates showed **huge** interest in it. After **discussing** it with his teachers, he was allowed to miss math class and instead spend time on the computer. His **aim** was to be able to write his own computer **programs**. Gates became not just a **brilliant** computer programmer but also a smart businessman. In 1975, before he finished university, Gates co-founded Microsoft. As the company became successful, Gates had no **reason** to finish his university studies. In 2015, the company **celebrated** its 40th birthday and is now the world's largest computer software company.

◀ **Bill Gates**

1. _____ (n) a goal; something you want to achieve

2. _____ (n) a statement that explains "why"

3. _____ (adj) very smart

4. _____ (v) to do something special for an important event

5. _____ (v) to become an adult

6. _____ (adj) very big

7. _____ (n) a set of instructions that tell a computer what to do

8. _____ (v) to talk about something

B List three ideas for each category below. Then share your ideas with a partner.

USING VOCABULARY

1. three things you **celebrate** every year

   _____   _____   _____

2. three **reasons** to study English

   _____   _____   _____

3. three **brilliant** scientists

   _____   _____   _____

C Skim the reading on pages 12–13. Who is the reading about? What was her great achievement? Check your ideas as you read the passage.

SKIMMING

THE MOTHER OF COMPUTING

🎧 Track 2

A   On October 16 every year, people celebrate Ada Lovelace Day. But who is Ada Lovelace, and what is she famous for?

B   When people think of the history of computers, they usually think of men such as Bill Gates and Steve Jobs. These men had a huge effect on the world of computing. But many historians believe the world's first computer programmer was a woman: Lady Augusta Ada King, also known as Ada Lovelace.

C   Ada Lovelace was born in 1815 and grew up in London, England. Her mother was a mathematician[1] and, as a young girl, Lovelace was brilliant at math and science. At the age of 13, she even created a design for a flying machine.

D   When she was 17 years old, Lovelace met a mathematician named Charles Babbage. They became friends and enjoyed discussing math together. At the time, Babbage was working on a design for a machine called an "Analytical Engine." The machine would be able to work on difficult math problems. Lovelace was very interested.

E   In 1843, Lovelace helped write an article on the Analytical Engine. She added her own ideas and notes to it. One of her notes described a step-by-step calculation[2] that the Analytical Engine could perform. Today, the Analytical Engine is thought to be the first design of what we now call a computer. And Lovelace's step-by-step calculation is thought to be the first ever computer program.

F   Ada Lovelace was one of very few female mathematicians and scientists in her time. Today, more women and girls study math and science than ever before, but they are still a minority.[3] One reason may be that the most famous mathematicians and scientists are men. The aim of Ada Lovelace Day is to celebrate the achievements of women in science, engineering, and mathematics. In this way, Ada Lovelace continues to be a role model[4] for young women around the world.

[1]A mathematician is someone who studies math.
[2]You make a calculation when you find out a number using math.
[3]A minority of people or things is fewer than half of them.
[4]A role model is a person who inspires others.

▲ A model of Charles Babbage's Analytical Engine

▲ A painting of Ada Lovelace in Whitechapel Art Gallery, London

UNDERSTANDING THE READING

A Why has Ada Lovelace become a role model?

    a. She is an example of someone who never gave up during difficult times.

    b. She came from a poor family but became a brilliant mathematician.

    c. She is a woman who made a great achievement in science and mathematics.

B Complete the summary with information from the reading on pages 12–13.

Ada Lovelace lived during the ^{1}_____ century. Her mother was a ^{2}_____. When Lovelace was ^{3}_____ years old, she met a man named ^{4}_____. He was designing a machine that could do ^{5}_____ problems. Lovelace was very interested. In 1843, Lovelace helped to write an article about the machine. She added her own ideas and notes. The machine is considered one of the first designs of a ^{6}_____, and Lovelace's notes are thought to be the first ever ^{7}_____. People who want the world to remember Lovelace created a day to celebrate her. Ada Lovelace Day is on ^{8}_____ every year.

C Note answers to the questions below. Then discuss with a partner.

1. In paragraph C, what adjective does the author use to describe Lovelace's math and science ability?

    _____

2. In the final sentence of the reading passage, what phrase does the author use to describe his/her opinion of Ada Lovelace?

    _____

3. In paragraph E, what evidence does the author give to support his/her opinion?

    _____

    _____

D What are three things that al-Jazari and Ada Lovelace have in common? Write your ideas below. Then discuss with a partner.

    _____

    _____

    _____

Writing

EXPLORING WRITTEN ENGLISH

A Read the information in the box.

> **LANGUAGE FOR WRITING** Simple Past Tense
>
> Use the simple past to talk about completed actions in the past.
>
> Ada Lovelace **lived** in London, England.
>
> Add -ed to the base form of a regular verb to form the simple past.
>
> invent—invent**ed**
>
> Add -d if the verb already ends in -e.
>
> live—live**d**   translate—translate**d**
>
> Make spelling changes for some verbs.
>
> For verbs that end in consonant + -y, drop the -y and add -ied:
>
> try—tr**ied**   study—stud**ied**   carry—carr**ied**
>
> For most verbs that end in consonant + vowel + consonant, double the final consonant and add -ed.
>
> stop—stop**ped**   excel—excel**led**   rob—rob**bed**
>
> Some verbs have irregular past forms.
>
> become—became   build—built   come—came   eat—ate
>
> find—found   go—went   grow—grew   have—had
>
> make—made   meet—met   put—put   say—said
>
> For negative statements, use did not (didn't) + the base form of a verb.
>
> She **didn't invent** the Analytical Engine.

Now write the simple past form of each verb below.

Base Form	Simple Past Form
create	
try	
say	
have	
design	
save	

Base Form	Simple Past Form
begin	
invent	
build	
grow up	
go	
discover	

B Complete the paragraphs with the simple past form of each verb in parentheses.

1. Hungarian László Bíró _____ (*invent*) the first ballpoint pen in the early 20th century. Bíró's brother _____ (*help*) him with the invention. Bíró and his brother were born in Hungary, but they _____ (*go*) to Argentina in 1943. Bíró _____ (*die*) in 1985.

2. In 1903, inventor Mary Anderson _____ (*have*) an idea. She noticed that car drivers _____ (*need*) to open their windows when it rained so that they _____ (*can*) see. Anderson _____ (*create*) a swinging rubber arm that drivers could control by using a lever inside a car. The invention was very popular and _____ (*become*) known as the windshield wiper.

3. Archaeologists _____ (*find*) the world's first bars of soap in Babylon, in modern-day Iraq. Babylonians_____ (*mix*) animal fat with wood ashes and water to make the soap.

C Look at the reading on pages 12–13 to answer the questions. Write complete sentences. Use the simple past.

1. When did Ada Lovelace live?

    _____

2. Where did she grow up?

    _____

3. What did her mother do?

    _____

4. What did she create when she was 13?

    _____

5. Who did she meet when she was 17?

    _____

    _____

6. When did she write the first ever computer program?

    _____

    _____.

A portrait of Ada Lovelace, by Alfred Edward Chalon

D Read the information below. Then complete each sentence (1–8) with the correct simple past form of *be*.

Use the simple past of *be* to describe people, things, and situations in the past. The verb *be* is usually followed by a noun, an adjective, or a prepositional phrase.

Ada Lovelace **was** *a mathematician.*

She **was** *talented.*

Lovelace and Babbage **were** *in London when they met.*

The past forms of *be* are *was/was not* and *were/were not*. You can use contractions for the negative forms: *wasn't* and *weren't*. We usually use contractions when we speak. We do not often use contractions in academic writing.

Ada Lovelace **was not** *a university professor.*

There **were not** *many female mathematicians in Lovelace's time.*

1. Ada Lovelace _____ good at math.

2. She and Charles Babbage _____ friends.

3. Charles Babbage _____ a mathematician.

4. There _____ many female scientists in Lovelace's time.

5. Lovelace's mother _____ a computer programmer.

6. Al-Jazari _____ an engineer.

7. Al-Jazari and Ada Lovelace _____ doctors.

8. Al-Jazari's elephant clock _____ small.

E Write true sentences (1–4) about famous people in the past. Use the past tense of *be*. Write two affirmative sentences and two negative sentences.

1. _____

2. _____

3. _____

4. _____

WRITING TASK

> **GOAL** You are going to write sentences on the following topic:
> Explain why we should have a day to celebrate a particular inventor.

PLANNING **A** Choose an inventor you know about. Make notes in the chart below.

Inventor's Name	What did he/she achieve? Why should we celebrate them?

FIRST DRAFT **B** Use your notes to write five sentences about the inventor. Use the simple past.

Main idea	I think we should celebrate _____.
Where / When was this person born?	He / She was born _____.
Main reason to celebrate this person	We should celebrate him / her because _____ _____ _____
A second reason	Also, _____ _____
What should people do on this day?	On this day, people should _____ _____ _____

EDITING **C** Now edit your draft. Correct mistakes with the simple past. Use the checklist on page 125.

UNIT REVIEW

Answer the following questions.

1. What are the simple past forms of these verbs?

   live _____   try _____   stop _____

   go _____   meet _____   build _____

2. What are some examples of modern day technology that use al-Jazari's ideas?

   _____

   _____

3. Do you remember the meanings of these words?
   Check (✓) the ones you know. Look back at the unit and review the ones you don't know.

   Reading 1:
   ☐ describe   ☐ drawing   ☐ engine
   ☐ engineer   ☐ float   ☐ history
   ☐ invent   ☐ machine   ☐ model
   ☐ sink

   Reading 2:
   ☐ aim   ☐ brilliant   ☐ celebrate
   ☐ discuss   ☐ grow up   ☐ huge
   ☐ program   ☐ reason

NOTES

When the base jumpers were ready, they jumped from the Jim Mao Tower in Shanghai, China.

OBJECTIVES **Grammar:** To learn about subordinating conjunctions
Vocabulary and Spelling: To study common words with the sound of **u** in w**oo**d
Writing: To write about an important day or time in your life

Can you write about an important day or time in your life?

Grammar for Writing

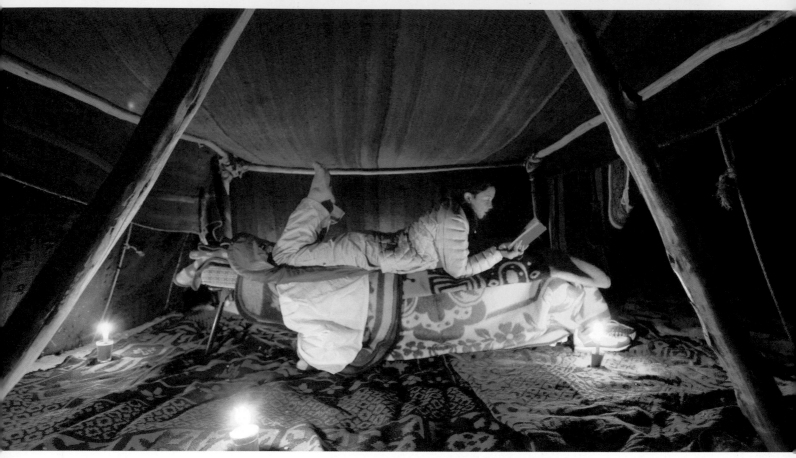

*Many people like to read a good book **before** they go to sleep.*

Subordinating Conjunctions: <u>because</u>, <u>after</u>, <u>before</u>, <u>when</u>, <u>if</u>

✓ The words **because, after, before, when,** and **if** are common conjunctions. They are very useful in good writing.

✓ These five words can connect two clauses. (A clause has a subject and a verb.)

✓ These five words connect two clauses to make a bigger sentence. The main clause (independent clause) can be a sentence all by itself.

✓ The dependent clause cannot stand by itself. The dependent clause needs the main clause to make sense. In other words, the dependent clause depends on the main clause.

Sentence	Main Clause	Dependent Clause
I failed the test **because** I did not study.	I failed the test	**because** I did not study.
Joe watches TV **after** he finishes dinner.	Joe watches TV	**after** he finishes dinner.
Many tourists need a visa **before** they can travel to the United States.	Many tourists need a visa	**before** they can travel to the United States.
People should be careful **when** they use a knife.	People should be careful	**when** they use a knife.
We will walk to class **if** the rain stops.	We will walk to class	**if** the rain stops.

Underline the main clause and put parentheses ( ) around the dependent clause.

Lim's Birthday

1. <u>I am going to bake a cake for Lim</u> (because tomorrow is his birthday).

2. I am going to make a chocolate cake because chocolate is his favorite kind of cake.

3. I need to go to the store before I can make Lim's cake.

4. I have to buy a lot of flour and sugar if I want to make a very big cake.

5. I can watch TV after I finish Lim's cake.

6. Lim is going to be so happy when he sees his birthday cake.

7. My brother will buy 26 candles for Lim's cake because Lim is going to be 26 years old.

8. My brother will put the candles on the cake when it is ready.

9. Lim's sister will sing Happy Birthday because she has a great voice.

10. Everyone will be happy if Lim is happy.

Word Order in Your Sentences

✓ The conjunctions **because, after, before, when,** and **if** often come in the middle of a sentence. The usual word order is <u>main clause</u> + <u>dependent clause</u>. The conjunction is part of the dependent clause.

Main Clause (S + V)	Dependent Clause (Conjunction + S + V)
John is hungry now	**because** <u>he</u> <u>did not eat</u> breakfast.

✓ It is also possible to begin a sentence with a dependent clause. In this case, the sentence begins with the conjunction **because, after, before, when,** or **if,** and you must use a comma after the dependent clause. The comma means the usual word order is not occurring.

✓ You do not use a comma before a dependent clause inside a sentence.

Dependent Clause (Conjunction + S + V)	Main Clause (S + V)
Because <u>John</u> <u>did not eat</u> breakfast,	he is hungry now.

✓ In a sentence with a noun and a pronoun, you use a noun the first time and a pronoun the second time. It does not matter which clause the noun or pronoun is in.

John is hungry now because **he** did not eat breakfast.

Because **John** did not eat breakfast, **he** is hungry now.

Underline the main clause and put parentheses ( ) around the dependent clause. Add a comma if the dependent clause comes before the main clause.

Lim's Birthday

1. (Because tomorrow is Lim's birthday), <u>I am going to bake a cake for him</u>.

2. Because chocolate is his favorite kind of cake I am going to make a chocolate cake.

3. Before I can make Lim's cake I need to go to the store.

4. I have to buy a lot of flour and sugar if I want to make a very big cake.

5. After I finish Lim's cake I can watch TV.

6. Lim is going to be so happy when he sees his birthday cake.

7. Because Lim is going to be 26 years old my brother will buy 26 candles for Lim's cake.

8. When the cake is ready my brother will put the candles on it.

9. Lim's sister will sing Happy Birthday because she has a great voice.

10. If Lim is happy his friends will be happy.

Using <u>because</u> in Your Writing

✓ The word **because** is used when you want to give a reason or explain something in the main clause.

✓ You can use **because** for the present, the past, or the future.

Time	Main Clause	Reason Clause (Dependent Clause with <u>because</u>)
present	I study every night	**because** I want to make good grades.
past	I failed the math test	**because** I did not understand the lesson.
future	I will study tonight	**because** we have a test tomorrow.

✓ When a sentence begins with a **because**-clause, you use a comma after the dependent clause.

✓ You do not use a comma if the main clause begins the sentence.

dependent clause　　　main clause	Use a comma.
Because it was expensive, Pablo did not buy it.	The dependent clause comes first.
main clause　　　dependent clause	Do not use a comma.
Pablo did not buy the car **because** it was expensive.	The dependent clause comes second.

ACTIVITY 3 **Using Commas with because**

Each pair of sentences has the same meaning. Add commas where necessary. Be ready to explain your answers.

1. a. You should wear a hat ☐ because it is sunny today.

   b. Because it is sunny today ☐ you should wear a hat.

2. a. Chinese is a difficult language for me ☐ because my language uses a different alphabet.

   b. Because my language uses a different alphabet ☐ Chinese is a difficult language for me.

3. a. It took me two weeks to read that book ☐ because it has 300 pages.

   b. Because that book has 300 pages ☐ it took me two weeks to read it.

4. a. Because Marie is from France ☐ she speaks French.

   b. Marie speaks French ☐ because she is from France.

5. a. Because it was so cold outside ☐ Ryan closed the window in his bedroom.

   b. Ryan closed the window in his bedroom ☐ because it was so cold outside.

6. a. We plan to live in Japan for one month ☐ because we want to learn Japanese.

   b. Because we want to learn Japanese ☐ we plan to live in Japan for one month.

7. a. Some people cannot eat cheese ☐ because they cannot have any milk products.

   b. Because some people cannot have any milk products ☐ they cannot eat cheese.

8. a. Giraffes are my favorite animal ☐ because they are very interesting.

   b. Because giraffes are very interesting ☐ they are my favorite animal.

ACTIVITY 4 **Writing Longer Sentences with because**

Combine the two sentences with **because** to make two longer sentences. Use pronouns to avoid repeating a noun. Be careful with capitalization, commas, and periods.

1. my sister will study tonight   she has a test tomorrow

   My sister will study tonight because she has a test tomorrow.

   Because my sister has a test tomorrow, she will study tonight.

2. you need an umbrella   it is raining now

   _____

   _____

3. the people understood the speaker easily   the speaker was excellent

_____

_____

4. my car is making a noise   I am taking my car to the repair shop

_____

_____

5. many irish families moved to america in the 1800s   life in ireland was difficult

_____

_____

6. the word **get** has many different meanings   the word **get** is difficult to use correctly

_____

_____

Using <u>after</u>, <u>before</u>, <u>when</u> in Your Writing

✓ The words **after, before,** and **when** are used in a time clause to explain the time relationship between the two clauses.

Conjunction	Main Clause	Time Clause (Dependent Clause with <u>after</u>, <u>before</u>, <u>when</u>)
after	I go home	**after** I finish my classes.
before	I eat breakfast	**before** I go to school.
when	I play computer games	**when** I have free time.

✓ When a sentence begins with **after, before,** or **when,** you use a comma.

✓ You do not use a comma if the main clause begins the sentence.

dependent clause main clause **Before** Pablo went to the airport, he did not call anyone.	Use a comma. The dependent clause comes first.
main clause dependent clause Pablo did not call anyone **before** he went to the airport.	Do not use a comma. The dependent clause comes second.

✓ **After** and **before** can also be prepositions. When a prepositional phrase begins a sentence, you usually use a comma.

prepositional phrase Pablo did not call anyone **before** his flight.	Do not use a comma. The prepositional phrase does not begin the sentence.
prepositional phrase **Before** his flight, Pablo did not call anyone.	Use a comma. The prepositional phrase begins the sentence.

ACTIVITY 5 Using Commas with after, before, when

Each pair of sentences has the same meaning. Add commas where necessary. Be ready to explain your answers.

1. a. Most children learn the names of the colors ☐ before they go to school.

   b. Before most children go to school ☐ they learn the names of the colors.

2. a. Jason went to work ☐ after he finished his breakfast.

   b. After Jason finished his breakfast ☐ he went to work.

3. a. When my father drives to work ☐ he listens to news on the radio.

   b. My father listens to news on the radio ☐ when he drives to work.

4. a. I added two cups of sugar ☐ after I added one cup of flour.

   b. After I added one cup of flour ☐ I added two cups of sugar.

5. a. When Jeff turned on the computer ☐ nothing happened.

   b. Nothing happened ☐ when Jeff turned on the computer.

6. a. My friends pushed my car ☐ when I could not start it.

   b. When I could not start my car ☐ my friends pushed it.

7. a. I wrote ten e-mails ☐ before I left the office.

   b. Before I left the office ☐ I wrote ten e-mails.

8. a. When we traveled from New York to Argentina ☐ the airline gave us dinner and breakfast.

   b. The airline gave us dinner and breakfast ☐ when we traveled from New York to Argentina.

ACTIVITY 6 Writing Two Longer Sentences with after, before, when

Combine the two sentences and the conjunction to make two longer sentences. Use pronouns to avoid repeating a noun. Be careful with capitalization, commas, and periods.

1. I heard your good news   I was so happy   when

   I was so happy when I heard your good news.
   _____

   When I heard your good news, I was so happy.
   _____

2. you should read the bill carefully   you pay the bill   before

   _____

   _____

3. we went to bed   we watched that long movie   after

_____

_____

4. I ate lunch   I washed my dish and put it in the cabinet   after

_____

_____

5. Natalia went to England   Natalia did not speak any English   before

_____

_____

6. my sister decided to buy those shoes   my sister saw the low price of those shoes   when

_____

_____

Using if in Your Writing

✓ Sometimes the main clause shows a result, and the dependent clause gives a condition, or a limit, for that result. In this case, the word **if** is used to show this condition relationship between two clauses.

Main Clause (The Result)	Dependent Clause with if (The Condition)
You cannot check your e-mail in this room	**if** the Internet does not work here.
You need six eggs	**if** you want to make a cake for ten people.
The passengers will miss their second flight	**if** their first flight arrives late.

✓ When a sentence begins with **if,** you use a comma. You do not use a comma when the main clause begins the sentence.

main clause dependent clause	Do not use a comma.
We will play basketball if we have extra time.	The dependent clause comes second.
dependent clause main clause	Use a comma.
If we have extra time, we will play basketball.	The dependent clause comes first.

ACTIVITY 7 **Using Commas with if**

Each pair of sentences has the same meaning. Add commas where necessary. Be ready to explain your answers.

1. a. If you eat more vegetables and less red meat ☐ you will be in better health.

    b. You will be in better health ☐ if you eat more vegetables and less red meat.

2. a. The answer to this question is 116 ☐ if you multiply the two numbers.

   b. If you multiply the two numbers ☐ the answer to this question is 116.

3. a. If a storm comes near our area ☐ you should listen to the radio.

   b. You should listen to the radio ☐ if a storm comes near our area.

4. a. Linda cannot eat this soup ☐ if there is meat in it.

   b. If there is meat in this soup ☐ Linda cannot eat it.

5. a. If you have any problems ☐ you should call me immediately.

   b. You should call me immediately ☐ if you have any problems.

6. a. If the weather is cold tomorrow ☐ everyone will need a heavy sweater.

   b. Everyone will need a heavy sweater ☐ if the weather is cold tomorrow.

ACTIVITY 8 **Writing Two Longer Sentences with _if_**

Read the two sentences and decide which is the **if**-clause (or condition clause) and which is the main (result) clause. Combine the two sentences with **if** to make two longer sentences. Use pronouns to avoid repeating a noun. Be careful with capitalization, commas, and periods.

1. my sister studies with her friends   she has an important test

   My sister studies with her friends if she has an important test.

   If my sister has an important test, she studies with her friends.

2. you read this book   you will laugh a lot

   _____

   _____

3. Rob can fix your computer   your computer is broken

   _____

   _____

4. The lake will freeze tonight   the weather is really cold

   _____

   _____

5. Sarah travels to China on November 16   the ticket will cost $1,500

   _____

   _____

6. I do not know the meaning of a word   I look up the meaning in a dictionary

_____

Common Student Mistakes

Student Mistake X	Problem	Correct Example ✓
You need a **sweater, because** the weather is cold.	comma before a dependent clause inside a sentence	You need a sweater **because** the weather is cold.
Because the weather is **cold you** need a sweater.	comma missing	Because the weather is cold**,** you need a sweater.
Because the weather is cold.	sentence fragment	**Because the weather is cold, you need a sweater.** OR **You need a sweater because the weather is cold.**

ACTIVITY 9 **Correcting Fragments**

The following sentences are fragments because they do not contain both a main clause and a dependent clause. Add information to make each sentence complete.

1. Because I need to learn English to get a better job.

I selected this school because I need to learn English to get a better job.

_____

OR

Because I need to learn English to get a better job, I selected this school.

_____

2. When I turned on the computer.

_____

3. Before everyone entered the office.

_____

4. If you work very hard this year.

_____

5. After you add the onions and the other vegetables to the pan.

_____

6. Because no one in my family speaks Spanish.

_____

7. When the weather in our area is very hot.

_____

8. Because my new phone is so hard to use.

_____

ACTIVITY 10 Scrambled Sentences

Change the order of the words to write a correct sentence. Be careful with spelling, capital letters, final punctuation, and word order. If there is a comma, it must stay with its word as shown. Do not add any commas.

Falling in Love with a New Pizza Restaurant

1. food is my favorite pizza

_____

2. because it pizza lot of has a i like cheese

_____

3. pizza night a went last a pizza, so eat restaurant wanted monday I to I

_____

4. was name the pizza the country restaurant of

_____

5. me about went country because a to pizza friend told it i

_____

6. I walked I had about the place when inside, a good feeling

_____

7. of restaurant looked menu had the many different kinds nice, and the pizzas

_____

8. the ten on the menu, kinds of pizza I order after I read about to decided the chicken pizza

_____

9. pizza, I was in love with this first piece of my when place tasted the I

_____

10. I recommend pizza pizza, want to if you eat a really delicious country

_____

ACTIVITY 11 **Finding and Correcting 10 Mistakes**

Circle the ten mistakes. Then write the sentences correctly. The number in parentheses ( ) is the number of mistakes in that sentence. Be ready to explain your answers.

Labneh and Provoleta

1. One of my favorite thing to eat is the cheese, and there are hundreds of different types of cheese. (2)

_____

2. When I was in Saudi Arabia, ate the labneh almost every day. (2)

_____

3. I like this creamy cheese, because it is has a good flavor and is low in calories (2)

_____

4. When were my family and I in Argentina, we ordered provoleta for dinner at least twice a week. (1)

_____

5. Argentineans grilled this thick cheese, and they use a fork and a knife to cut them just like a steak. (2)

_____

6. I like to eat all kinds of cheese, but labneh from the Saudi Arabia and provoleta from Argentina are my two favorite types of cheese. (1)

_____

_____

Track 3 •)) **ACTIVITY 12** **Dictation**

You will hear six sentences three times. Listen carefully and write the six sentences. The number in parentheses ( ) is the number of words. Be careful with capital letters and end punctuation.

1. _____ (8)

2. _____ (9)

3. _____ (9)

4. _____ (10)

5. _____ (15)

6. _____ (12)

Practicing Grammar and Vocabulary in Model Writing

Read the sentences in the paragraph very carefully. Fill in the missing words from the word bank. Circle the 33 letters that need to be capital letters. Add commas in the correct places. Then copy the paragraph on your own paper.

received	about	for	beginning	graduated	become	wanted
immediately	when	flew	important	enjoyed	advice	forget

An Important Day in My Life

1 this story is about an _____ day in my life. **2** in may 2009, i _____ from my university. **3** i studied education and i wanted to _____ a teacher. **4** i _____ to teach in brazil. **5** i looked on the internet for information _____ a job in brazil. **6** _____ i found a really good job posting i wrote an e-mail to the school. **7** on that day, i _____ a letter that offered me that job. **8** after i got that letter i talked to my family for their _____. **9** my parents liked this job a lot so i _____ accepted the job. **10** i _____ to sao paulo on august 24 and i started teaching there a week later. **11** i taught english in brazil _____ three years. **12** i _____ my time there very much. **13** i will never _____ august 24, 2009. **14** that day was the _____ of my teaching career in brazil.

Write the paragraph from Activity 13 again, but make the changes listed below and all other necessary changes.

Sentence 1. Add **very** in the correct place. You will need to change another word.

Sentence 3. Change **teacher** to a different profession. Change other words about teaching in other sentences.

Sentence 4 and others. Change **Brazil** to a different country.

Sentences 4 and 5. Combine the information in these two sentences with **because.** Use the word **there** instead of the country name the second time.

Sentence 6. Change **the school** to a place that fits with the change you made in Sentence 3.

Sentence 10. Change **Sao Paulo** to a city in the country you chose in Sentence 4. Combine the clauses with **when.**

Sentences 13 and 14. Combine these two sentences with **because.**

_____

_____

_____

_____

_____

_____

_____

_____

_____

_____

_____

_____

_____

_____

Building Vocabulary and Spelling

Learning Words with the Sound of $\boxed{u}$ in $\boxed{\text{wood}}$*

$\underline{u}$ = w $\underline{oo}$ d   This sound is usually spelled with the letters **oo, u, ou,** and another spelling.

wood

push

could

ACTIVITY 15 **Which Words Do You Know?**

This list has 22 common words with the sound of $\underline{u}$ in w$\underline{oo}$d.

1. Notice the spelling patterns.
2. Check ✓ the words you know.
3. Look up new words in a dictionary. Write the meanings in your Vocabulary Notebook.

Common Words

GROUP 1:
Words spelled with **oo**

☐ **1.** b o o k

☐ **2.** c o o k

☐ **3.** c o o k i e

☐ **4.** f o o t

☐ **5.** g o o d

☐ **6.** l o o k

☐ **7.** s t o o d

☐ **8.** t o o k

☐ **9.** w o o d

☐ **10.** w o o l

☐ **11.** u n d e r s t o o d

*List is from: Spelling Vocabulary List © 2013 Keith Folse

GROUP 2:
Words spelled with **u**

☐ 12. b u l l

☐ 13. b u s h

☐ 14. f u l l

☐ 15. p u l l

☐ 16. p u s h

☐ 17. p u t

☐ 18. s u g a r

GROUP 3:
Words spelled with **ou**

☐ 19. c o u l d

☐ 20. s h o u l d

☐ 21. w o u l d

GROUP 4:
Other spelling

☐ 22. w o m an

ACTIVITY 16   **Matching Words and Pictures**

Use the list in Activity 15 to write the common word that matches the picture.

1. _____   3. _____

4.

2. _____   4. _____

5. _____   7. _____

6. _____   8. _____

ACTIVITY 17 **Spelling Words with the Sound of <u>u</u> in w<u>oo</u>d**

Fill in the missing letters to spell words with the sound of <u>u</u> in w<u>oo</u>d. Then copy the correct word.

1. b __ k   _____   6. p __ ll   _____

2. s __ gar   _____   7. underst __ d _____

3. f __ ll   _____   8. g __ d   _____

4. l __ k   _____   9. f __ t   _____

5. w __ l   _____   10. p __ t   _____

Writing Sentences with Vocabulary in Context

Complete each sentence with the correct word from Activity 17. Then copy the sentence with correct capital letters, commas, and end punctuation.

1. the plural of .... is feet

   _____

2. do you want me to .... some milk and .... in your tea

   _____

3. our new boss is .... of new ideas for the company

   _____

4. the .... on the table belongs to carlos

   _____

5. you should never .... a plug from an outlet by its cord

   _____

6. the weather is cold so it is .... for you to wear a heavy .... sweater

   _____

7. maria thomas and amina .... all the words on the test yesterday so their scores were very high

   _____

   _____

8. zebras .... like horses with stripes

   _____

ACTIVITY 19 **Scrambled Letters**

Change the order of the letters to make a word that has the sound of <u>u</u> in w<u>oo</u>d.

_____	1. o o k c	_____	8. d o w o
_____	2. s h u p	_____	9. o w m a n
_____	3. o u s h l d	_____	10. b o k o
_____	4. s h u b	_____	11. k o t o
_____	5. i e c o o k	_____	12. w u o l d
_____	6. t o d o s	_____	13. g u r s a
_____	7. u o c l d	_____	14. n d r s t d u e o o

ACTIVITY 20 **Spelling Practice**

Write the word that you hear. You will hear each word two times.

1. _____   6. _____   11. _____

2. _____   7. _____   12. _____

3. _____   8. _____   13. _____

4. _____   9. _____   14. _____

5. _____   10. _____ 15. _____

ACTIVITY 21 **Spelling Review: Which Word Is Correct?**

This review covers the different ways of spelling **u** in w**oo**d in this unit. Read each pair of words. Circle the word that is spelled correctly.

	A	B		A	B
1.	book	buk	11.	full	ful
2.	coukie	cookie	12.	should	shuld
3.	bull	boul	13.	good	gud
4.	cuod	could	14.	look	lok
5.	wuman	woman	15.	stod	stood
6.	couk	cook	16.	wod	wood
7.	pute	put	17.	boll	bull
8.	tuk	took	18.	wuld	would
9.	pul	pull	19.	sagur	sugar
10.	fut	foot	20.	wool	wol

ACTIVITY 22 **Spelling Review**

Read the four words in each row. Underline the word that is spelled correctly.

	A	B	C	D
1.	bax	box	boox	boux
2.	lenguaje	lenguaje	languaje	language
3.	meny	meany	many	mny
4.	sead	sed	sayed	said

	A	B	C	D
5.	funny	funni	funie	funy
6.	laymun	laimun	lemon	lemun
7.	estop	stob	stop	stap
8.	auful	auwful	aweful	awful
9.	plis	pliss	plese	please
10.	suger	sugar	shugar	shuger
11.	everything	evrithing	everythng	evrithng
12.	wumun	wumen	womun	women
13.	never	neaver	niver	neiver
14.	happen	hoppen	hepen	hapen
15.	could	culd	coold	cuold
16.	famos	famoso	femous	famous
17.	practike	practis	practice	proctice
18.	estudent	estuden	studen	student
19.	bicos	bicause	becos	because
20.	tuk	tok	toake	took

Original Student Writing

Writing Your Ideas in Sentences or a Paragraph

Write six to twelve sentences on your own paper. Write about an important day or time in your life. (You can also write about the first time you did something, such as flew on an airplane, gave a speech in public, or got a pet.) Combine clauses with subordinating conjunctions. For help, you can follow the examples in Activity 13 and Activity 14.

Peer Editing

Exchange papers from the above activity. Read your partner's sentences.
Then use Peer Editing Sheet 1 on ELTNGL.com/sites/els to make comments about the writing.

NOTES

ALIEN WORLDS 3

A spotted porcupinefish swims along the ocean floor.

THINK AND DISCUSS

1 Which do you think is more interesting—the ocean or space? Why?

2 Do you think it's more useful to explore the ocean or space? Why?

A Look at the information on these pages and answer the questions.

1. What is the Milky Way? What do we know about it?
2. In which part of the Milky Way do we live?
3. What does the Milky Way look like when seen from Earth?

B Use the correct form of the words in blue to complete the sentences.

Our _____ is called Earth.

Earth has just a _____ moon, while Jupiter has 67.

The sun is a _____ .

0°

1

10,000

SCUTUM ARM

20,000

SAGITTARIUS A

60°

PERSEUS

30,000

90°

ARM

50,000 light-years

40,000

Direction of rotation

120°

OUTER

150°

OUR HOME IN SPACE

The Milky Way Galaxy—our home—has hundreds of billions of **stars**. Our solar system—which includes the sun, Earth, Mars, Venus, and other **planets**—is in a part of the galaxy called the Orion Arm. The solar system may seem big to us, but it is a small part of our galaxy. Light from one end of the galaxy would take 100,000 years to travel to the other side. However, the Milky Way is just a **single** galaxy, and it is small compared to the universe. Astronomers—scientists who study space—think there are billions of galaxies beyond our Milky Way.

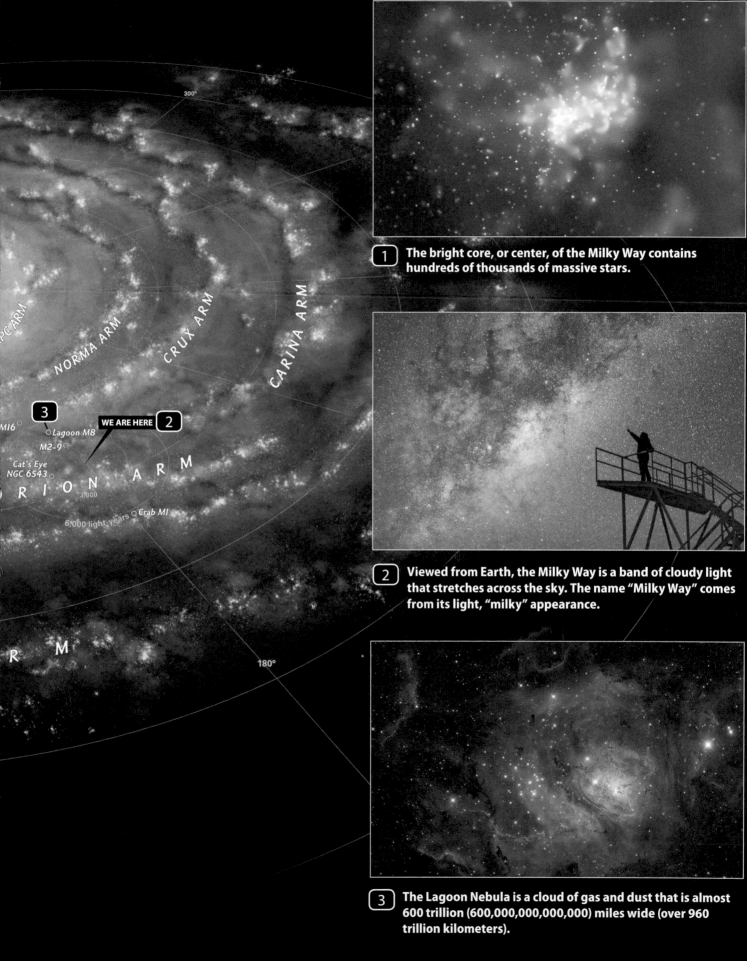

300°

PC ARM

NORMA ARM

CRUX ARM

CARINA ARM

3

MI6°

○ Lagoon M8

WE ARE HERE   2

M2-9○

Cat's Eye
NGC 6543○

R I O N   A R M

3,000

6,000 light-years ○ Crab MI

R   M

180°

1 The bright core, or center, of the Milky Way contains hundreds of thousands of massive stars.

2 Viewed from Earth, the Milky Way is a band of cloudy light that stretches across the sky. The name "Milky Way" comes from its light, "milky" appearance.

3 The Lagoon Nebula is a cloud of gas and dust that is almost 600 trillion (600,000,000,000,000) miles wide (over 960 trillion kilometers).

Reading 1 QUICK READ SEE PAGE 116

PREPARING TO READ

BUILDING
VOCABULARY

A The words in **blue** below are used in the reading passage on pages 47–48. Match the correct form of each word with its definition.

> At a **distance** of around 60 million kilometers, Mercury is the **nearest** planet to the sun.
>
> Scientists believe that in the past, conditions on Mars may have been **suitable** for **life**.
>
> It takes around eight minutes for light from the sun to **reach** Earth.
>
> Astronomers **discovered** the dwarf planet Pluto in 1930.
>
> Scientists are **excited** by the fact that there is an ocean of water beneath the surface of Saturn's moon Enceladus.

1. _____ (v) to find something for the first time

2. _____ (v) to arrive at

3. _____ (adj) very interested and happy

4. _____ (adj) right for something

5. _____ (adj) close, not far

6. _____ (n) the amount of space between two things

7. _____ (n) things that are alive

USING
VOCABULARY

B Answer the questions below with a partner. Use the diagram at the bottom of the page to help.

1. Which **planet** is the biggest in the solar system?

2. Which is **nearer** the sun: Mars or Venus?

3. Why do you think conditions on Pluto are not **suitable** for **life**?

PREVIEWING

C Read the first paragraph of the reading on pages 47–48. What two questions does the author ask? What do you think the answers to these questions are? Discuss your ideas with a partner.

The Solar System

Mercury · Earth · Jupiter · Saturn · Uranus · Neptune · Venus · Mars · Pluto

An artist's idea of the surface of an exoplanet in the Trappist-1 star system

OTHER WORLDS

🎧 Track 5

A   Look up at the sky on a dark, moonless night. There are many thousands of **stars**. But are there other **planets** like Earth? And could humans live there one day?

B   New technology is helping astronomers **discover** hundreds of new planets. So far, we know of more than 3,500 "exoplanets." These are planets that move around stars other than the sun. Some exoplanets may be similar to Earth.

C   An Earthlike exoplanet must have certain features.[1] It needs to be the right **distance** from its star. It will then have a **suitable** temperature for living things: not too cold and not too hot. A planet at the right distance from its star might also have water. Where there is water, there might also be **life**.

D   Recent discoveries have shown that Earthlike exoplanets may be more common than once thought. In 2016, scientists were **excited** to find seven Earthlike exoplanets around a **single** star—Trappist-1. Each planet is a similar size to Earth, and each may have water. Although the seven planets are all very close to the star, Trappist-1 is much cooler than our sun. Temperatures could therefore be suitable for life.

[1] A **feature** of something is an interesting or important part of it.

In the future, a starship like this might carry thousands of people to a new home planet.

E   Could it be possible for humans to live on an Earthlike planet one day? The biggest problem is distance. The **nearest** star system, Alpha Centauri, is 4.3 light-years[2] from Earth. In 2016, scientists found an Earthlike exoplanet in this system. However, traveling there with today's technology would take thousands of years.

F   With future technology, however, this may change. Scientist Andreas Tziolas thinks that one day we might be able to travel to another star system. He thinks that new technology will let us **reach** the nearest star in a few decades.[3] "I believe we can achieve some form of interstellar[4] exploration within a hundred years," he says.

[2] A **light-year** is the distance that light travels in one year. It equals about 9.46 trillion (9,460,000,000,000) kilometers.
[3] A **decade** is 10 years.
[4] If something is **interstellar**, it occurs between two or more stars.

UNDERSTANDING THE READING

A Match each of these main ideas with a paragraph (B–F) from the reading.

_____ 1. Traveling to exoplanets is difficult because they are very far away.

_____ 2. Exoplanets that are similar to Earth might have water and maybe even life.

_____ 3. Astronomers have found many exoplanets.

_____ 4. Scientists found seven Earthlike exoplanets around the same star.

_____ 5. In the future, new technology may allow humans to travel to an exoplanet.

B Answer the questions. Circle the correct option.

1. What is an exoplanet?
   a. a planet that is similar in size to Earth
   b. a planet that moves around a star outside our solar system

2. According to the passage, what is true about Alpha Centauri?
   a. It is the closest star system to Earth.
   b. It has more Earthlike exoplanets than any other star system.

3. What does Andreas Tziolas believe?
   a. We already have the technology to travel to Alpha Centauri.
   b. Travel to another star system will be possible in the future.

C Complete the notes about the Trappist-1 star system.

The Trappist-1 star and its seven exoplanets

- The system contains seven exoplanets that are a similar size to ¹_____.
- The planets are very ²_____ to the star, but Trappist-1 is very ³_____ compared to other stars.
- The planets may have ⁴_____ and therefore possibly life.

CRITICAL THINKING   **Speculation** involves making a guess or prediction. It is important to identify which parts of an article are speculation and which are facts.

D Read the following sentences from the article. Check (✓) the sentences that are speculation. Circle the words that helped you decide.

☐ 1. New technology is helping astronomers discover hundreds of new planets.
☐ 2. Earthlike exoplanets may be more common than once thought.
☐ 3. Trappist-1 is much cooler than our sun.
☐ 4. Temperatures could therefore be suitable for life.
☐ 5. One day we might be able to travel to another star system.

DEVELOPING READING SKILLS

READING SKILLS Taking Notes

Taking notes as you read can help you remember important information in a passage. It will also help you remember key ideas for a writing task or test.

As you read, note key nouns, such as names, places, and times. Include details about each one. Also, note how ideas and information relate to each other. For example, note any causes and effects, problems and solutions, steps in a process, or events in a story. Remember that when you write notes, you don't need to write complete sentences.

It can be helpful to note information using an outline or a graphic organizer. Here is one example:

> <u>Outline</u>
>
> **Main Idea**
> > *Detail*
> > *Detail*
>
> **Main Idea**
> > *Detail*
> > *Detail*

TAKING NOTES **A** Complete the outline using information from pages 47–48.

p. 47 para B
- **Main Idea:** astronomers use new _____ to find exoplanets
- **Detail:** so far, found more than _____
- **Detail:** some may be like _____

p. 48 para E
- **Main Idea:** main problem with traveling to an exoplanet is _____
- **Detail:** nearest star system is _____ away
- **Detail:** traveling there would take _____ years

APPLYING **B** Now create your own outline for paragraph F on page 48.

- **Main Idea:**

- **Detail:**

- **Detail:**

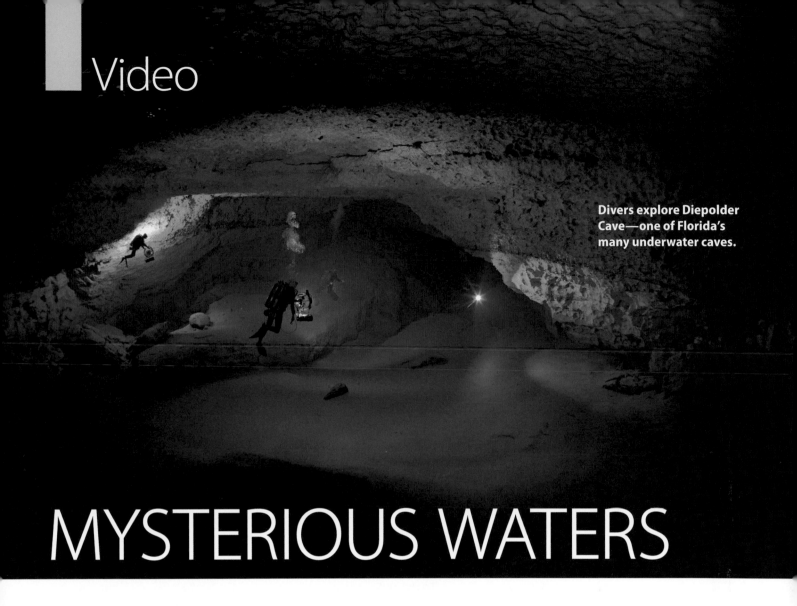

Video

Divers explore Diepolder Cave—one of Florida's many underwater caves.

MYSTERIOUS WATERS

BEFORE VIEWING

A Look at the photo and read the caption. Where are the people? What do you think they can learn from exploring a place like this? Discuss your ideas with a partner.

DISCUSSION

B The words in **bold** below are used in the video. Match the correct form of each word to its definition.

VOCABULARY IN CONTEXT

> An echo is created when sound **bounces** off a surface and returns to the listener.
>
> It's hard to swim in water that has a strong **current** because it can push you in the wrong direction.
>
> An underwater cave system can be like a **labyrinth**. It is very easy to get lost.
>
> A **three-dimensional** (3D) map of a city shows how tall the buildings are.

1. _____ (adj) not flat, having a shape
2. _____ (n) water moving in one direction
3. _____ (n) a place in which it's difficult to find your way, like a maze
4. _____ (v) to hit a surface and then quickly move away from it

C Read the information about the Wakulla Springs cave system. Then answer the questions.

Florida's Wakulla Springs is one of the largest underwater cave systems in the world. When it was first explored in 1955, explorers found the bones of land animals that lived thousands of years ago. They also found a number of items that belonged to humans. The explorers realized that a long time ago, the area was above sea level. As the caves filled with water, the animal bones and other objects were kept safe for thousands of years.

1. What two things did divers find when the caves were first explored?

_____

2. What did this tell the explorers about the area?

_____

WHILE VIEWING

A ▶ Watch the video. What was the purpose of the team's dive?

a. to look for the bones of ancient animals

b. to study animal species living in the caves

c. to create a map of the caves

B ▶ Watch the video a second time and complete the notes.

- Diving can be very [1]_____: Around [2]_____ divers have died in Florida's caves since 1960.

- Boyd Matson makes a mistake: kicks up a lot of [3]_____ and can't see. Uses a [4]_____ to get out.

- Divers use a machine to [5]_____ sound waves off the cave walls to create a 3D map.

- Deep in the cave, the [6]_____ is very strong. But in the end, the divers return safely to the surface. The dive is successful.

AFTER VIEWING

A Would you like to explore underwater caves? Why or why not? Note your ideas below. Then discuss with a partner.

_____

_____

B How are the challenges of exploring underwater similar to the challenges of exploring space? Note your ideas below. Then discuss with a partner.

_____

_____

_____

Reading 2 QUICK READ SEE PAGE 119

PREPARING TO READ

A The words in **blue** below are used in the reading passage on pages 54–55. Complete the definitions using the correct form of the words.

> Most of space is a **mystery** to us. We don't know much about it.
> A layer of gray dust **covers** the moon.
> You have to use a special **vehicle** to explore **deep** parts of the ocean.

1. _____ (n) something that you cannot explain or understand
2. _____ (n) a machine that moves people or things from one place to another
3. _____ (v) to make a layer over the top of something
4. _____ (adj) far below the surface of something

B Read the definitions below. Then complete each sentence with the correct word.

> A **variety** is a number of different kinds or examples of something.
> An **illness** is a disease, or a period of being sick.
> If you **complete** a task or a journey, you finish it.
> The **beginning** of something is the first part of it.

1. There are a _____ of reasons that people decide to study space.

2. In 1840, the British explorer Sir James Clark Ross used a tool to get samples from the ocean floor. Some believe this was the _____ of deep-sea exploration.

3. You should not go swimming if you have an _____ like a cold or the flu.

4. In 22 years, the space shuttle Columbia _____ 27 flights into space.

C List three ideas for each category below. Then share your ideas with a partner.

1. three animals that live **deep** in the ocean

_____ _____ _____

2. three **vehicles** that are used in water

_____ _____ _____

3. three common **illnesses**

_____ _____ _____

D You are going to read an article about deep-sea exploration. Why do you think it might be useful to explore the deepest parts of the oceans? Work with a partner and list some ideas. Then read the passage to see which of your ideas are mentioned.

HIDDEN DEPTHS

🎧 Track 6

A Oceans have always seemed mysterious. In the past, people believed that giant dragons and other monsters lived deep in the seas. Other people imagined mermaids[1] and underwater cities.

B Today, much of the world's oceans are still a mystery. "The oceans cover 71 percent of our planet," says oceanography[2] professor Dr. Robert Ballard. "Yet only 5 percent of it has been explored." In fact, we know more about some areas of Mars than about some parts of the world's oceans.

MOUNTAINS IN THE SEA

C New technology, however, is helping scientists explore these hidden worlds. For example, scientists are using an underwater vehicle called DeepSee to explore seamounts—underwater mountains.

D Scientists have used DeepSee to study Las Gemelas, an area of seamounts near Costa Rica. A huge variety of species lives on and around Las Gemelas. Some of these species have never been seen before. Some may have chemicals that can help people fight illnesses, such as cancer.

DOWN IN THE DEPTHS

E The deepest place on Earth is the Mariana Trench in the Pacific Ocean. The ocean floor there is about 36,000 feet (11,000 meters) deep. In 2012, filmmaker and explorer James Cameron reached the Mariana Trench in a vehicle called Deepsea Challenger. He was the first person to complete the journey alone. Cameron took photos and video on the ocean floor. He also collected underwater samples.[3]

F Vehicles such as Deepsea Challenger are helping us discover new animals and plants. Some of these have been around for millions of years. These discoveries could help us better understand how life on our planet began. Deep-sea exploration also helps us in other ways. For example, we are learning how underwater earthquakes cause tsunamis.[4] As Cameron says, "This is the beginning of opening up [a] new frontier."[5]

[1] In stories, a **mermaid** is a woman with a fish's tail who lives in the ocean.
[2] **Oceanography** is the study of the ocean.
[3] A **sample** is a small amount of something that shows you what the rest is like.
[4] A **tsunami** is a very large wave that can cause damage on land.
[5] A **frontier** is a place that people are just starting to explore.

Some strange creatures live in the deepest parts of the oceans, such as the frilled shark (top), viperfish (middle), and giant spider crab (bottom).

The underwater vehicle DeepSee explores a seamount in Las Gemelas.

UNDERSTANDING THE READING

UNDERSTANDING
THE GIST

A Which of the following would be the best alternative title for the reading?

a. Deep-Sea Discoveries   b. Saving Sea Creatures   c. Underwater Earthquakes

UNDERSTANDING
DETAILS

B Complete the notes about the reading passage.

(Paras A and B) Oceans = mystery

cover _____ of Earth

expl'd _____

we know more about _____

(Paras C and D) New tech. → explore more

vehicle called _____

went to _____ near _____

(Paras E and F) Deepest place in ocean = _____

2012: _____ explored alone

he took _____ and collected _____

deep-sea exploration helps us understand how _____

also learn about how _____ cause _____

CRITICAL THINKING:
GUESSING MEANING
FROM CONTEXT

C The words below are synonyms—words with similar meanings—of words in the reading passage. Scan the reading to find the correct synonyms.

1. (Paragraph A) dreamed _____

2. (Paragraph C) unseen _____

3. (Paragraph F) findings _____

CRITICAL THINKING:
ANALYZING AN
ARGUMENT

D Note answers to the questions below using information from the reading passage.

1. What do ocean scientists and explorers study underwater?

_____

_____

2. Why is their work useful? (What are some possible benefits?)

_____

_____

CRITICAL THINKING:
SYNTHESIZING

E Look back at your answer to question 1 on page 43. Has your opinion changed? Complete the sentence and list two reasons. Share your ideas in a small group.

I think _____ exploration is more interesting.

Reason 1: _____

Reason 2: _____

Writing

EXPLORING WRITTEN ENGLISH

A Read the information below.

LANGUAGE FOR WRITING Introducing Your Opinion

You can use the verbs *think* and *believe* to introduce an opinion about something.

I think *we can reach Mars someday.*
I don't think *we can ever reach Mars.*
I believe *we can learn a lot by studying space.*
I don't believe *we can learn much by studying space.*

You can also use the phrase *in my opinion*. Remember to use a comma after *in my opinion.*

In my opinion, *humans will need to move to another planet one day.*
In my opinion, *humans won't be able to live on Earth forever.*

Now complete the sentences (1–6). Use positive or negative forms to give your own opinion. Use the correct forms of the words in parentheses in the last two sentences (5–6).

think / don't think

1. I _____ many humans will live on another planet 50 years from now.

2. I _____ scientists will discover life on Mars.

believe / don't believe

3. I _____ it's important to spend a lot of money on space exploration.

4. I _____ governments should spend more money on exploration than on education.

In my opinion, / In my opinion, . . . not

5. _____, space exploration (*be*) _____ important.

6. _____, astronomers (*have*) _____ a more interesting job than ocean explorers.

NASA's Curiosity rover captured this image from the surface of Mars.

B Write your opinion about each of the ideas below. In each sentence, use a different phrase to introduce your opinion.

Example: *Space exploration can help us learn about our own planet.*
<u>I believe space exploration can help us learn about our own planet.</u>

1. Studying the ocean is a waste of time and money.

   _____

2. Life forms from other planets are looking for us.

   _____

3. People will live on an exoplanet 100 years from now.

   _____

C Read the information below.

LANGUAGE FOR WRITING Using Modal Verbs to Make Predictions

You can use modals to make predictions about the future. For example, you can use *will* to make predictions you are sure about. Use *may* and *might* to make predictions you are less sure about.

   *Any mission to Mars **will** be very expensive.* (certain)
   *Underwater exploration **may** help us understand how life began.* (less certain)
   *Traveling to another world **might** be possible in the future.* (less certain)

Remember: Use the base form of the verb after a modal verb.

To make a negative statement, add *not* after the modal verb.

   *There **might not** be a mission to Mars before 2050.*

Now unscramble the words and phrases to make sentences.

1. in tall apartment buildings / will / in the future / live / I think / most people /.

   _____

2. be / cities like / New York and Beijing / even more crowded / might /.

   _____

3. apartment buildings / people / leave / might never / their / need to /.

   _____

4. most people / in my / home / opinion, / work / from / will /.

   _____

D Circle the best option to complete each sentence.

1. I **will** / **might** not be able to play soccer this weekend. I'll let you know by Friday.
2. I heard it **will** / **may** snow tomorrow. The weatherman said there's a 50 percent chance.
3. There's no way that we **will** / **might** ever live on Jupiter.
4. I **will** / **may** come to the party, but I haven't decided yet.
5. Next year, my birthday **will** / **might** be on a Tuesday.

EDITING PRACTICE

Read the information. Then find and correct one mistake in each of the sentences.

In sentences with *may, might,* and *will,* remember:
- to use the base form of the verb.
- to use *will* for things you are sure about. Use *may* or *might* when you are not sure.

1. Robots may replaced doctors someday.

2. I think people will having computers inside their bodies in the future.

3. Someday, we might to build homes underground.

4. I believe new telescopes will finding many more exoplanets in the future.

5. We will be able to see Saturn in the sky tonight. It depends if the skies are clear.

Radio telescopes in Chile observe the night sky.

WRITING TASK

> **GOAL** You are going to write sentences on the following topic:
> Express your opinion about the future of space or ocean exploration.

PLANNING **A** Make notes in the chart below using information from this unit. Add ideas of your own.

Astronomers study space because . . .	Ocean scientists study the sea because . . .

FIRST DRAFT **B** Use your ideas to answer this question: *What should governments spend more money on—space exploration or ocean exploration?* Use opinion expressions and *will*, *might*, and *may*.

Main idea	_____ governments should spend more money on _____ exploration than _____ exploration.
Reason 1	With _____ exploration, we can learn more about _____.
Reason 2	Also, _____.
Reason 3	Finally, _____ because _____.

EDITING **C** Now edit your draft. Correct mistakes with modal verbs. Use the checklist on page 125.

UNIT REVIEW

Answer the following questions.

1. What are two phrases you can use to introduce your opinion?

   _____

2. What can people learn by studying the deepest parts of our oceans?

   _____

   _____

3. Do you remember the meanings of these words? Check (✓) the ones you know. Look back at the unit and review the ones you don't know.

   Reading 1:
   ☐ discover   ☐ distance   ☐ excited
   ☐ life   ☐ near   ☐ planet
   ☐ reach   ☐ single   ☐ star
   ☐ suitable

   Reading 2:
   ☐ beginning   ☐ complete   ☐ cover
   ☐ deep   ☐ illness   ☐ mystery
   ☐ variety   ☐ vehicle AWL

NOTES

Astronaut Tracy Caldwell Dyson looks out of the window of the International Space Station.

OBJECTIVES To learn the simple future tense with *be going to* and *will*
To practice time words to show the future
To learn complex sentences in the future
To study articles *a*, *an*, and *the*
To use *because* in complex sentences

Can you write about what you think will happen in the future?

The Simple Future Tense: *Be Going To*

We use the **simple future tense** to talk about future events. One way to express the simple future tense is to use *be going to*. You can use *be going to* for:

- plans that are already made

- predictions (guesses about the future) that are about the possible result of actions that are happening in the present

Subject	Be Going To		Verb (Base Form)
I	am		eat
he / she / it	is	going to	study
			buy
we / you / you (plural) / they	are		listen
✗ I am going to a sandwich for lunch.			
✓ I am going to buy a sandwich for lunch.			
✗ According to the radio report, the weather going to be severe tonight.			
✓ According to the radio report, the weather is going to be severe tonight.			

ACTIVITY 1 **Making Predictions**

Make a prediction about the actions in each picture. Write complete sentences using the correct form of *be going to*.

1. _____

   _____

   _____

   _____

   _____

   _____

2. _____

   _____

   _____

   _____

   _____

   _____

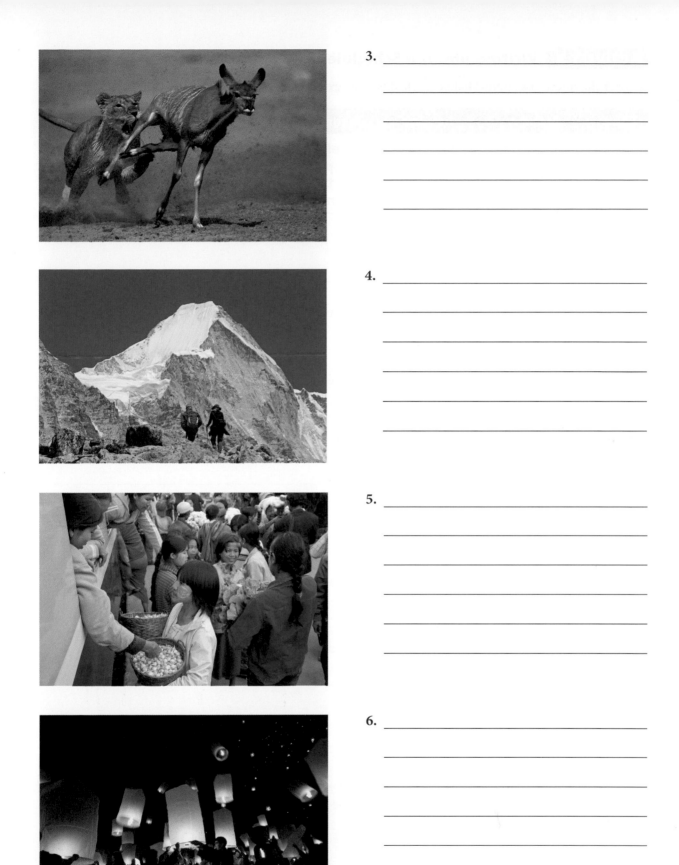

3. _____
   _____
   _____
   _____
   _____
   _____

4. _____
   _____
   _____
   _____
   _____
   _____

5. _____
   _____
   _____
   _____
   _____
   _____

6. _____
   _____
   _____
   _____

ACTIVITY 2 **Writing about a Schedule**

Answer the questions about Michael's schedule for next week. Use complete sentences.

Sunday	Monday	Tuesday	Wednesday	Thursday	Friday	Saturday
meet Mom & Dad for lunch	meeting with Mr. Anderson	appointment with Mr. & Mrs. Pinter at the office	business report due to Ms. Simms	buy groceries	dinner with Andrea	play soccer with the guys

1. What is Michael going to do on Sunday?

   _____

2. Who is going to come to Michael's office on Tuesday?

   _____

3. On what day are Michael and Andrea going to have dinner?

   _____

4. When is Michael going to meet with Mr. Anderson?

   _____

5. What is he going to do on Thursday?

   _____

6. What are Michael and his friends going to do on Saturday?

   _____

7. What is he going to give to Ms. Simms on Wednesday?

   _____

Writer's Note

Avoiding *Gonna* in Writing

Speakers of English often pronounce *going to* as *gonna* in informal speech. However, do not use *gonna* in academic writing. You must write out the words completely.

✗ I'm gonna buy a new shirt.

✓ I am going to buy a new shirt.

Grammar for Writing

The Simple Future Tense: *Will*

Another way to express the simple future tense is to use **will**. You can use *will* for:

- future plans/decisions that are made at the moment of speaking (no planning)
- strong predictions (strong guesses about the future)
- promises and offers to help

Subject	*Will*	Verb (Base Form)
I		eat
you		study
he / she / it	will	buy
we		run
you (plural)		listen
they		

✗ I will opens the door for you.
✓ I will open the door for you.

✗ They will are watch a new movie tonight.
✓ They will watch a new movie tonight.

✗ We will be love each other forever.
✓ We will love each other forever.

Using Adverbs of Frequency with *Will*

Adverbs of frequency describe how often an action happens. Some examples are *always, sometimes, often, rarely,* and *never*. When you use frequency adverbs with *will*, put the frequency adverb between *will* and the main verb.

✗ My parents always will help me.
✓ My parents will always help me.

✗ The teacher will give us sometimes homework.
✓ The teacher will sometimes give us homework.

ACTIVITY 3 Writing about the Future Using *Will*

Make five predictions about what your life will be like in ten years. Use *will* in the sentences. Use a frequency adverb in two sentences.

1. _____

2. _____

3. _____

4. _____

5. _____

Grammar for Writing

Time Words and Phrases

Good writers include **time words** and **time phrases** in their writing. Time words and phrases give important information about *when* something happens.

Common Time Words and Phrases			
first	in a minute	tomorrow	next week
next	later	next Saturday	next year
then	before that	next January	next time
finally	after that		

These time words usually occur at the very beginning or the very end of a sentence. When the time words and phrases occur at the beginning of a sentence, a comma is usually used.

We are going to go to the movies **on Saturday**.

On Saturday, we are going to go to the movies.

The airline will produce a new kind of jet **in the next few months**.

In the next few months, the airline will produce a new kind of jet.

We are going to paint the kitchen **first**.

First, we are going to paint the kitchen.

NOTE: *Then* is not followed by a comma.

ACTIVITY 4 Practicing with Time Words

Fill in the missing time words from the word bank. One word can be used twice. Add commas where necessary.

> then   next   first   after   Sunday   finally

Example Paragraph 1

A Reunion to Remember

This year's family reunion will be special because we are going to celebrate my Aunt Laura's 98th birthday. **1** _____ everyone in our family is going to travel to my aunt's town for the weekend. The **2** _____ night, we are going to meet at Aunt Laura's house and eat a delicious dinner. **3** _____ dinner, we are going to bring out a delicious birthday cake.

4 _____ we will sing to her and give her presents. She is
going to love it! The **5** _____ day, the whole family will
meet in the city park for a lovely picnic. There will be food, games, and
music for everyone. Aunt Laura will give a nice speech to the family,
too. On **6** _____ everyone will go to lunch with Aunt
Laura. **7** _____ our special celebration will be over, and
everyone will return home dreaming about next year's reunion.

Review the sentences you wrote about Michael's schedule in Activity 2. Put them in correct time order, starting with Sunday. Write the sentences in paragraph form below. Use some time words to help organize your sentences.

Example Paragraph 2

Michael's Busy Schedule

      Michael is *going to* be a very busy man next week. First, he is *going to* meet his mom and dad for lunch on Sunday.

_____

_____

_____

_____

_____

_____

_____

_____

_____

_____

Finally, he is *going to* play soccer with his friends on Saturday. Michael is the busiest man I know!

Writer's Note

Will vs. Be Going To

Will and *be going to* are both ways to form sentences about the future. There are certain situations when a writer may use only *will* or only *be going to* because the situation has a specific meaning. However, *will* and *be going to* can often be used to talk about the future with little or no difference in meaning.

When writing an essay or a report, remember that *will* is more formal and more common in academic writing than *be going to*. As you write, be careful to consider whether the situation requires using *will, be going to,* or either.

Underline the 10 future tense verbs in the paragraph below. (Hint: Two of them might be difficult to find.) Then answer the questions that follow using complete sentences.

Carmen's Fifteenth Birthday

Next week, Carmen Viera will be 15 years old, and her family has plans for a special celebration for her. On her birthday, Carmen is going to wear a beautiful white **gown**. First, she is going to go to church with her family and friends. After church is over, they will go to an **elegant ballroom**. Then they are going to have a party called a *quince* there. When Carmen arrives, she will perform some formal dances with her friends. After that, everyone is going to dance, eat, and celebrate. Carmen can **hardly** wait. She knows that she will always remember her special day.

a gown: a long, formal dress

elegant: graceful; refined

a ballroom: a large room where formal parties are held

a *quince*: the Spanish word for *fifteen*; a traditional Latin birthday party that celebrates when a girl becomes a woman

hardly: almost not; with difficulty (a negative word)

Post-Reading

1. How old will Carmen be next week?

_____

2. What is Carmen going to wear on her birthday?

_____

3. What is the first thing she is going to do on her birthday?

   _____

4. Where will they hold her *quince* party?

   _____

5. What will Carmen and her friends do at the party?

   _____

Grammar for Writing

The Simple Future Tense: Negatives

Add the word *not* to make the simple future tense (*be going to* and *will*) negative.

Subject	Be	Not	Going To	Verb (Base Form)
I he / she / it we / you / you (plural) / they	am is are	**not**	going to	eat study buy run listen
✗ Sara not going to take me to the airport on Sunday. ✓ Sara is not going to take me to the airport on Sunday. ✗ Brett and Erica no going to play soccer tomorrow. ✓ Brett and Erica are not going to play soccer tomorrow.				

Subject	Will	Not	Verb (Base Form)
I you he / she / it we you (plural) they	will	**not**	eat study buy run listen
✗ They will not to come to the party. ✓ They will not come to the party. ✗ The president not make a speech on television tonight. ✓ The president will not make a speech on television tonight. ✗ My company will don't give me a raise this year. ✓ My company will not give me a raise this year.			

Writer's Note

Contractions with the Simple Future Tense

Several contractions are possible in the simple future tense.

Will

I will = I'll   we will = we'll

you will = you'll   they will = they'll

he / she / it will = he'll / she'll / it'll

will not = won't

Be Going To

I am going to = I'm going to   we are going to = we're going to

you are going to = you're going to   they are going to = they're going to

he / she / it is going to = he's / she's / it's going to

are not = aren't

is not = isn't

Remember to ask your instructor if using contractions in this course is acceptable.

ACTIVITY 7 Changing Affirmative to Negative

Rewrite the affirmative sentences as negative sentences, and rewrite the negative sentences as affirmative ones. Write out the entire sentence.

1. There will not be a test on this information soon.

   _____

2. Our friends are not going to meet us at the mall this weekend.

   _____

3. Angela is going to leave for work soon.

   _____

4. Our plane will leave the airport on time.

   _____

5. I am going to write an e-mail to my friends back home.

   _____

6. The temperature will drop sharply this evening.

   _____

7. That little boy will not eat his spinach.

   _____

Answer the questions.

1. What is one important thing that you are going to do in your life?

   _____

   _____

2. How long will it take to do it?

   _____

3. What are you going to do to reach this goal? Write at least three things.

   _____

   _____

   _____

   _____

4. How will you feel when you reach this goal? Why?

   _____

   _____

Grammar for Writing

Verbs in Complex Sentences about the Future

Use the simple present tense and the simple future tense with complex sentences about the future.

Clause 1 (Simple Future)	Clause 2 (Connector + Simple Present)
Calvin **is going to take** a nap	<u>after</u> he **finishes** his work.
Those birds **will fly** south	<u>before</u> the weather **becomes** too cold.

Clause 1 (Connector + Simple Present)	Clause 2 (Simple Future)
<u>If</u> we **do not leave** now,	we **will be** late.
<u>When</u> Maya **gets** home,	she **is going to read** a good book.

Do <u>not</u> use the simple future tense in both clauses.

    ✗ When the rain <u>is going to stop</u>, I am going to rake the leaves.

    ✓ When the rain stops, I am going to rake the leaves.

    ✗ The police will arrest a passenger on the plane after Flight 873 <u>will arrive</u> in Paris.

    ✓ The police will arrest a passenger on the plane after Flight 873 arrives in Paris.

Identify each sentence as a simple (*S*), compound (*CD*), or complex (*CX*) sentence. If the sentence is compound or complex, insert a comma if necessary.

1. _____S_____ I am going to go surfing next weekend.

2. _____CD_____ My father is going to retire next year, but my mother is going to continue working.

3. _____CX_____ After Gerardo finishes painting, his house will look beautiful.

4. _____ Irene is going to call you when she gets home from work.

5. _____ Brett and his friends are going to go to the hockey game and cheer for their team.

6. _____ Ariel is going to go to college next year but her brother is going to get a job.

7. _____ When the game is over we are going to eat at Harvey's Grill.

8. _____ I will bring a salad and dessert to the party.

9. _____ Leslie and Serena will be roommates next semester but they do not get along very well.

10. _____ If we do not finish this project on time the company will lose the contract.

11. _____ Ana and her friends will not be able to go to the museum this weekend.

12. _____ We are going to visit our family in Mexico City next weekend.

Answer each question using a complex sentence with connectors such as *after, before, when, until,* and *as soon as.* Use the correct verb tense in each clause.

1. What are you going to do after you graduate?

_____

2. What are you going to do as soon as you finish this activity?

_____

3. What will you not do before you go to bed tonight?

_____

4. When are you going to do your homework?

_____

5. When will you finish all your English courses?

_____

6. What are you going to do after you eat dinner?

_____

Writer's Note

Using the Future Tense in Academic Writing

Writers may use the future to make a prediction about the information in their academic writing. Therefore, it is common to find the future tense in the last sentence of a paragraph. The future can also be used to describe a process. However, it is rare to find an entire academic paragraph that only uses the future tense.

Grammar for Writing

The Indefinite Articles: *A/An*

A, an, and *the* are three of the shortest words in English, but they are also three of the most important words. These words are called **articles**. They are very important in correct writing and speaking.

The **indefinite articles** *a* and *an* can only be used with singular count nouns. You learned the following rules:

- Use *a* or *an* in front of a singular count noun when the noun is general (not specific).
- Use *a* in front of a singular count noun that begins with a <u>consonant</u> sound.

- Use *an* in front of a singular count noun that begins with a <u>vowel</u> sound. Some words beginning with *h* and *u* have exceptions to this rule.

    I bought **a** sweater.

    Luis is going to eat **a** red apple.

    Wendy has **an** elegant home.

The Definite Article: *The*

The definite article *the* can be used with both singular and plural count nouns and also with non-count nouns.

- Use *the* for the second (and third, fourth, etc.) time you talk about something.

    I bought a sweater and a coat yesterday. **The sweater** is made of wool, but **the coat** is made of leather. **The sweater** was cheap, but **the coat** was expensive.

- Use *the* when the speaker and the listener both know about or are familiar with the subject.

    My brother called and said, "I'm locked out of **the house**."

- Use *the* when the noun you are referring to is unique—there is only one. This thing can be natural or manmade.

    The Sun and **the Earth** are both in **the Milky Way Galaxy**.

    The Eiffel Tower is a beautiful monument.

    I am going to visit **the Sidney Opera House** next summer.

    The New Caledonia Barrier Reef is an important home for green sea turtles.

Article Use Summary

When Your Meaning Is:	Singular Count Nouns	Plural Count Nouns	Non-count Nouns
General	a / an	Ø*	Ø*
Specific	the	the	the

*Ø means "do not use an article."

Using Modifiers with Singular Count Nouns

A non-count noun (*water, honesty*) and a plural count noun (*cars, women*) can be used alone in a sentence. However, a singular count noun (*car, woman*) cannot be used alone in a sentence. These words must always be preceded by a modifier (a word that gives more information about the noun).

- an article (*a, an, the*)
  - ✗ April owns computer.
  - ✓ April owns a computer.
- a possessive adjective (*my, your, his*)
  - ✗ I am reading book.
  - ✓ I am reading my book.
- a quantifier (*one, another, some*)
  - ✗ Give me spoon. This one is dirty.
  - ✓ Give me another spoon. This one is dirty.

There are more examples of quantifiers on page 145 in the *Brief Writer's Handbook*.

ACTIVITY 11 **Practicing Articles**

Fill in the blanks with *a, an,* or *the*. If no article is needed, write Ø.

Example Paragraph 4

A World Traveler

Robert likes to travel a lot, and next year he is going to go on

1 _____ excellent trip. **2** _____ trip is going to be

to Egypt and New Zealand. He wants to meet **3** _____

many new people and try **4** _____ interesting food. While

he is in Egypt, he is going to see **5** _____ Great Pyramids

at Giza and **6** _____ Sphinx of Cheops. He wants to take

7 _____ cruise down **8** _____ Nile River, but

it is probably going to be too expensive. After he visits Egypt, he will

fly to New Zealand to visit **9** _____ cousin who lives there.

10 _____ his cousin's name is Thomas. Robert and Thomas

are going to hike along the coast of New Zealand for a few weeks.

They want to see **11** _____ tuatara. Tuataras are lizards

from **12** _____ ancient reptile family. Because tuataras are

nocturnal, it is going to be difficult to see them. Finally, they will take

13 _____ bike trip on **14** _____ country's North

Island. **15** _____ trip will **definitely** be memorable!

nocturnal: active at night

definitely: without any doubt or question; surely

ACTIVITY 12　Review: Sentence Writing

Write complete sentences using the words below. Do not change the order of the words. Add the correct article(s) (*a, an, the*) where necessary. Use the correct verb tense, punctuation, and capitalization.

1. robert / not go / to / beach / tomorrow

   _____

2. laura's parents / visit / taj Majal / in india / next month

   _____

3. we / have / grammar test / next week

   _____

4. weather / be / very / nice / for / picnic / this saturday

   _____

5. kate and brad / meet / friend / for dinner / tomorrow

   _____

6. I / lend / you / some money / until / you / get your paycheck

   _____

7. this / computer / not work / anymore

   _____

8. I / bring / apple pie / for dessert

_____

9. after nicholas / graduate next week / his sister / give him / expensive gift

_____

10. my dad / meet / me / at airport / when / I / arrive / from algeria

_____

Grammar for Writing

Complex Sentences with *Because*

How would you answer this question: *Why did you decide to study English?*

One common way to answer a *why* question is to use a complex sentence with the connector *because*.

Clause 1: Includes Part of the Question	Clause 2: *Because* + Reason (Answer)
They are going to study English	**because** they want to learn a second language.
	because they want to study in an English-speaking country.
	because they like the way it sounds.

Fragments with *Because*

In formal writing, the *because* clause must be part of a complex sentence; it cannot be used as a stand-alone sentence. If the *because* clause is used as a stand-alone sentence, it is a fragment and is a mistake.

(fragment)
✗ We are not going to go to the beach. Because it is raining.

(complex sentence)
✓ We are not going to go to the beach because it is raining.

(fragment)
✗ Megan is going to go to the bookstore. Because she needs to buy a book.

(complex sentence)
✓ Megan is going to go to the bookstore because she needs to buy a book.

Because can also be used at the beginning of a sentence. When it is, you must put a comma at the end of the *because* clause.

✗ Because his brother broke the computer Alan got angry.

✓ Because his brother broke the computer, Alan got angry.

ACTIVITY 13 Identifying Sentences vs. Fragments

Identify each group of words as a complete sentence (*S*) or a fragment (*F*). If it is a complete sentence, add correct capitalization and punctuation.

1. ___S___ D̶ante passed the test because he studied hard.

2. ___F___ because the weather was so bad on Saturday evening

3. _____ because it will be cold in the mountains we are packing our heavy jackets

4. _____ because everyone will have a wonderful time at the party

5. _____ because he is going to forget about his appointment

6. _____ she is going to arrive late because her car broke down

7. _____ because I live in new york I go to the theater on broadway often

8. _____ because some committee members will not attend the conference

9. _____ the computers are going to be down today because a storm knocked out the power

10. _____ because the managers are out of the office we are going to postpone the meeting

ACTIVITY 14 Writing Sentences with *Because*

Answer each question using a complex sentence with *because*. Use the correct verb tense.

1. Why are you studying English?

   _____

2. Why is soccer a popular sport?

   _____

3. Why is fast food becoming popular around the world?

   _____

4. Why are you going to study in the library for your next test?

   _____

5. Why do some people like to drive fast?

_____

6. Why do you like your hobby?

_____

7. Why do you write letters to your family?

_____

8. Why did you skip breakfast this morning?

_____

9. Why do children learn to print before they learn cursive writing?

_____

10. Why did the man stop at the food cart?

_____

Writer's Note

Paying Attention to Commas

It is very important to pay attention to commas in your writing. Ask yourself *why* you are using a comma in the sentence. If you cannot explain the rule, the comma probably does not belong in the sentence. Every time you write, take a moment to review all your commas.

There is a list of common comma rules on pages 140–141.

ACTIVITY 15 Practicing Comma Rules

For each item, combine the two sentences into one sentence. Remember the comma rules for compound sentences, complex sentences, and lists. You may have to change or delete some words. Be prepared to explain the comma rule that you use.

1. At the party, we ate food. We talked with our friends, and we played games.

_____

_____

_____

2. First, we are going to go to the store. Then we are going to make dinner.

_____

_____

_____

3. John wants to go to the movies. Rob and Theo want to go home.

_____

_____

_____

4. I lived in Lahore when I was a child. Lahore is in Pakistan.

_____

_____

_____

5. Elizabeth will not ride roller coasters. Roller coasters are too scary.

_____

_____

_____

ACTIVITY 16 Editing: Grammar and Sentence Review

Correct the paragraph. There are 11 mistakes.

2 capitalization mistakes
1 adjective mistake
2 missing verbs

4 missing commas
1 misused comma
1 misused article

Example Paragraph 5

My Winter Vacation

My winter vacation is going to be wonderful, because I am going to go to quebec. I am going to go there with my best friend. We going to spend one week in the city, and then we are going to explore the countryside for a week. I have the aunt who lives there, and she going to show us all the sights beautiful. We do not speak french very well so we are a little bit nervous. After I arrive in Canada I am going to buy a lot of souvenirs for my parents brother and friends. I cannot wait for my vacation to begin!

Building Better Vocabulary

ACTIVITY 17　Word Associations

Circle the word or phrase that is most closely related to the word or phrase on the left. If necessary, use a dictionary to check the meaning of words you do not know.

	A	B
1. a reunion	many animals	many friends
2. presents	attendance	gifts
3. a speech	you can eat it	you can hear it
4. to celebrate	to have fun	to have problems
5. formal	very common	very proper
6. to forget	I cannot graduate	I cannot remember
7. hardly	very difficult	almost not at all
8. angry	a negative feeling	a positive feeling
9. to hike	to run	to walk
10. honesty	lies	truth
11. few	not near	not many
12. ancient	very new	very old
13. nocturnal	awake during the day	awake at night
14. a vacation	a time for fun	a time for work
15. a cousin	your uncle's child	your mother's child

ACTIVITY 18　Using Collocations

Fill in each blank with the word that most naturally completes the phrase on the right. If necessary, use a dictionary to check the meaning of words you do not know.

1. building / vacation　　an ancient _____

2. about / for　　to forget _____ something

3. between / along　　to drive _____ the coast of Nova Scotia

4. sight / animal　　a nocturnal _____

5. honest / unique   a(n) _____ experience

6. ballroom / speech   an informative _____

7. formal / honest   this is a(n) _____ event

8. sights / souvenirs   to visit all the _____

9. honest / angry   to get _____

10. speech / cruise   to attend a _____

ACTIVITY 19   **Parts of Speech**

Study the word forms. Fill in each blank with the best word form provided. Use the correct form of the verb. If necessary, use a dictionary to check the meaning of words you do not know. (NOTE: The word in bold is the original word that appears in the unit.)

Noun	Verb	Adjective	Sentence Practice
anger	anger	**angry**	1. She is going to be _____ when I tell her the news.
			2. The children _____ their mother yesterday.
honesty	Ø	honest	3. Please give me an _____ answer.
			4. _____ is the best policy.
nerve / nervou<u>ness</u>	Ø	**nervous**	5. Ben was _____ about taking the exam.
			6. I can see the _____ in her expression.
formal<u>ity</u>	formal<u>ize</u>	**formal**	7. The dance next week is going to be _____.
			8. Meeting the new university president is only a _____.
unique<u>ness</u>	Ø	**unique**	9. The _____ of the Hungarian language makes it difficult to learn.
			10. The style of Emma's dress is definitely _____.

Noun endings: -y, -ness, -ity

Verb ending: -ize

Adjective ending: -y

Original Student Writing

ACTIVITY 20 **Original Writing Practice**

Reread the paragraph on Carmen Viera in Activity 6 on page 71. Then review your answers to Activity 8 on page 74. Use the information from Activity 8 to write about an event that is going to happen to you in the future.

Follow these steps for writing. Put a check (✓) next to each step as you complete it. When you finish your paragraph, use the checklist that follows to edit your work.

_____ STEP 1: In your first sentence, tell who you are and what you are going to do in the future.

_____ STEP 2: In the next two sentences, give more details to describe what you are going to do.

_____ STEP 3: In the next four or five sentences, describe how you are going to achieve this goal.

_____ STEP 4: In the last sentence, tell why it is important for you to achieve this goal. (Use the word *because* in the final sentence.)

_____ STEP 5: Use time words, such as *after* and *as soon as*, in some of your sentences in STEP 3.

_____ STEP 6: Write at least one compound and one other complex sentence in your paragraph.

_____ STEP 7: Use at least two of the vocabulary words or phrases presented in Activity 17, Activity 18, and Activity 19. Underline these words and phrases in your paragraph.

If you need ideas for words and phrases, see the Useful Vocabulary for Better Writing on pages 149–151.

☑ Checklist

1. ❏ I used *be going to* or *will* when talking about the future.

2. ❏ I used articles correctly in my sentences.

3. ❏ I used commas correctly.

4. ❏ I checked that each sentence has a subject and a verb—there are no fragments!

5. ❏ I gave my paragraph a title.

ACTIVITY 21 **Peer Editing**

Exchange papers from Activity 20 with a partner. Read your partner's paragraph. Then use Peer Editing Sheet 2 on ELTNGL.com/sites/els to help you comment on your partner's paragraph. Be sure to offer positive suggestions and comments that will help your partner improve his or her writing. Consider your partner's comments as you revise your own paragraph.

Additional Topics for Writing

Here are ten ideas for journal writing. Choose one or more of them to write about. Follow your teacher's directions. (We recommend that you skip a line after each line that you write. This gives your teacher a place to write comments.)

PHOTO TOPIC: Look at the photo on pages 62–63. Write about what you think will happen in the future. For example, write about the future of space travel. What planets are humans going to visit? What things are going to be discovered in space? Do you think that humans will be able to live on other planets?

TOPIC 2: Write about something that you plan to do in the next two weeks. Include the people who are going to be with you, where you are going to be, and why you are going to do this.

TOPIC 3: Write about something that you plan to do in the next six months. Be sure to include where this activity is going to happen, who is going to be with you, and why you chose this activity.

TOPIC 4: Choose a current topic in the news. Read about it. Then write about what you think will happen and tell why.

TOPIC 5: Think about a special project or event that is going to happen in your neighborhood, city, or country. What is going to happen? When will it happen? Why is it happening? When will this project finally be completed?

TOPIC 6: Write about what you are going to do before you return home today. Make a list: Who are you going to be with? Are you going to do this thing (or these things) for work, school, or pleasure? How long is it going to take you to complete these things?

TOPIC 7: Describe what your wedding will be like. How big will the wedding party be? Who will be there? Where will it happen?

TOPIC 8: Describe the job you want to have when you finish school. What kind of job is it? What are your responsibilities going to be in this job? Are you going to work for a company or for yourself? How much money are you going to earn in this job?

TOPIC 9: Write about what you plan to study (your major) in college. Why did you choose this subject? What classes are going to be easy for you, and what classes are going to be difficult? How long is it going to take you to get your degree?

TOPIC 10: Describe what life is going to be like in the year 2050. What new things are going to be available? How is life going to be better than it is now? How is life going to be worse than it is now?

Timed Writing

How quickly can you write in English? There are many times when you must write quickly, such as on a test. It is important to feel comfortable during those times. Timed-writing practice can make you feel better about writing quickly in English.

1. Take out a piece of paper.

2. Read the writing prompt below.

3. Brainstorm ideas for five minutes.

4. Write eight to ten sentences.

5. You have 20 minutes to write.

Describe something that you plan to do next year. Be sure to include who is going to be with you, where it is going to happen, and why you are going to do this.

_____

_____

_____

_____

_____

_____

_____

_____

_____

_____

Adverbs

A boy gently blows bubbles at an iguana in Pevas, Peru.

OBJECTIVES **Grammar:** To learn about adverbs
Vocabulary and Spelling: To study common words with the sound of <u>ow</u> in fl<u>ow</u>er
Writing: To write about a person you know

Can you write about a person you know?

Grammar for Writing

On Monday and Tuesday, Camilla works **at a restaurant.** She is **very** tired, but she **always** does her job **carefully.**

What Is an Adverb?

✓ An **adverb** is a word that adds more information to a sentence.

sentence	I answered the difficult question.
more interesting sentence	adverb of manner adverb of degree adverb of place adverb of time I **correctly** answered the **most** difficult question in math class yesterday.

✓ An adverb can be a single word (**yesterday**) or a prepositional phrase used as an adverb (**in math class**).

✓ There are five main kinds of adverbs: **place, time, manner, frequency,** and **degree.** Each kind of adverb does a different job in a sentence.

     time   degree   frequency   place   manner
At 5 a.m., my **very** big cat **usually** jumps on my bed, and I **quickly** open my eyes.

✓ **Adverbs of place** tell <u>where</u>.
  here, there, in this room

✓ **Adverbs of time** tell <u>when</u>.
  now, then, in the morning

✓ **Adverbs of manner** tell <u>how</u>.
  quickly, well, carefully

✓ **Adverbs of frequency** tell <u>how often</u>.
  always, never

✓ **Adverbs of degree** tell <u>how much</u>.
  very, so, extremely

ACTIVITY 1 Finding Adverbs in Sentences

Find and circle these 30 adverbs in the sentences. The number in parentheses is the number of adverbs in the sentence.

well	usually	after the news	incredibly	in our next check
so	early	in my car	carefully	between two other cars
late	loudly	at 7 a.m.	quickly	after breakfast
really	there	last month	in a hurry	to my office
never	very	extremely	at work	at our company
already	on time	at 5 a.m.	yesterday	in the meeting

More Money for Me

1. We had a (very) special meeting at our company yesterday, so I had to get up early. (4)

2. At 5 a.m., my alarm clock rang loudly, and I quickly opened my eyes. (3)

3. I usually take my time eating breakfast, but I ate my breakfast in a hurry. (2)

4. After breakfast, I got in my car and drove to my office. (3)

5. I arrived at work at 7 a.m. and carefully parked my car between two other cars. (4)

6. All of the other office workers were already there. (2)

7. My co-workers never arrive late, so we were able to begin the meeting on time. (3)

8. In the meeting, our boss told us some incredibly good news. (2)

9. We will receive a special bonus in our next check for working so well last month. (4)

10. After the news, everyone was extremely happy and really talkative. (3)

Adverbs of Place and Time

✓ **Adverbs of place** tell <u>where</u>.

> My new apartment is **here,** but my old apartment was **near the lake.**

✓ **Adverbs of time** tell <u>when</u>.

> Joe and I watched a movie **last night.** It ended **at 10 p.m.**

✓ The most common location for an adverb of place or time is near the end of a sentence.

>   place   time
> Queen Elizabeth II was born **in London.** She was born **in 1926.**

✓ If a sentence has both an adverb of place and an adverb of time, the adverb of place usually comes before the adverb of time. (Hint: Remember that P for <u>place</u> comes before T for <u>time</u> in the alphabet.)

>   place   time
> Queen Elizabeth II was born **in London in 1926.**

✓ An adverb of place or time can also begin a sentence, but you usually put a comma to separate it from the subject of the sentence.

✓ You do not usually use a comma after a one-word adverb such as **here** or **yesterday.**

place	**In France,** people put sugar on their popcorn.
	On the second floor of the house, there are three bedrooms and one bathroom.
	Here you can see a map of China. (no comma)
time	**In 1926,** Queen Elizabeth II was born in London.
	On January 30, 2012, Florida Bank opened a new office in downtown Miami.
	Yesterday we went to the bank and the post office. (no comma)

ACTIVITY 2   **Writing Two Sentences with Adverbs of Place and Time**

Change the order of the words to write two sentences. Be careful with capital letters, commas, and periods.

1. classes / my brother and sister / at 8 a.m. / begin / their

   My brother and sister begin their classes at 8 a.m.

   At 8 a.m., my brother and sister begin their classes.

2. in 2011 / were / in madrid / we

   _____

   _____

3. to the united states / jose / came / five years / martinez / ago

_____

_____

4. a pair of / at the mall / jonathan / yesterday / new / shoes / bought

_____

_____

5. are / at / going to eat / lucas / and / lunch / a steak restaurant / tomorrow / i

_____

_____

6. on / play / with maria / carla / saturday morning / i / tennis / and diana

_____

_____

Adverbs of Manner

✓ **Adverbs of manner** tell <u>how</u>.

> You should fry the meat **quickly** to keep the flavor.

✓ Most adverbs of manner consist of an adjective + **–ly**.

> adjective
> Lim is a very **careful** driver.
>
> adverb of manner
> Lim drives very **carefully.**

adjective	adverb	adjective	adverb
careful	carefully	quick	quickly
clear	clearly	quiet	quietly
current	currently	slow	slowly
easy	easily	sudden	suddenly

Exceptions: good → **well**; fast → **fast**; hard → **hard**

✓ The most common location for an adverb of manner is near the end of a sentence.

> adverb
> Our teacher spoke **clearly.**

✓ If there is an object, the adverb goes after the object.

> object   adverb
> He explained all **of the new vocabulary** **carefully.**

ACTIVITY 3 **Writing Adjectives and Adverbs of Manner in Three Sentences**

Write each group of words as three complete sentences. Use the correct adjective or adverb. Be careful with capital letters, commas, and periods.

1. (quick) maria is a great student she always has a _____ answer maria answers _____

   Maria is a great student.   She always has a quick answer.

   Maria answers quickly.

2. (slow) paul is a _____ writer he likes to take his time paul writes _____

   _____

   _____

3. (good) mrs smith is a _____ teacher the students like her class a lot she explains things _____

   _____

   _____

4. (easy) i studied a lot for today's test it was an_____ test for me i answered everything _____

   _____

   _____

5. (careful) please read the questions _____ you need to understand the questions before you answer them you need to be a _____ reader

   _____

   _____

Adverbs of Frequency

✓ **Adverbs of frequency** tell <u>how often</u>.

> Kevin and I **never** eat lunch at noon. Our lunch is **always** at 11:30.

✓ Common adverbs of frequency include:

> **always   usually   often   sometimes   seldom   rarely   hardly ever   never**

✓ The most common location for an adverb of frequency is <u>after</u> the verb **be**, but <u>before</u> other verbs.

> I <u>am</u> **always** late to meetings.   I **always** <u>arrive</u> late to meetings.

✓ When a verb has two parts, the frequency word goes in the middle.

> I <u>can</u> **usually** <u>eat</u> a whole pizza.   People <u>should</u> **always** <u>lock</u> their doors.

✓ The word **sometimes** can occur at the beginning, middle, or end of a sentence.

beginning	**Sometimes** John and I watch TV at night.
middle	John and I **sometimes** watch TV at night.
end	John and I watch TV at night **sometimes**.

Writing Answers in Sentences with Adverbs of Frequency

Read each question and then write a sentence about yourself. Use an adverb of frequency. Use correct capital letters, commas, and periods.

1. Can you name something that you always do on Monday?

   I always wake up early on Monday.
   _____

2. What do you usually eat for breakfast?

   _____

3. Can you name something that you never eat for breakfast?

   _____

4. What is something that you seldom do in the morning?

   _____

5. What is something that your mother sometimes does on the weekend?

   _____

ACTIVITY 5 **Writing Interview Sentences Using Adverbs of Manner**

Use the five questions from Activity 4 to interview another student. On your own paper, write six sentences about that person.

Use this sentence for sentence 1: **This information is about _____.**

Then, your sentence 2 will be from question 1 in Activity 4. Your sentence 3 will be from question 2 in Activity 4, and so on.

In sentences 2 to 6, be sure to use an adverb of frequency with the information about the person you interviewed.

Use correct capital letters, commas, and periods.

Adverbs of Degree

✓ **Adverbs of degree** tell how much.

   The bus station was **very** crowded. It was **extremely** hot.

✓ Common adverbs of degree include:

   very   really   extremely   so   too   incredibly   completely

✓ The adverb of degree **too** has a negative meaning. It is not used with positive words.

   Negative meaning: The soup was **too** salty. (This use is correct.)

   Positive meaning: The soup was **too** delicious. (This use is NOT correct.)

✓ Adverbs of degree can come before an adjective or an adverb.

before an adjective	The test was **extremely** difficult.
before an adverb	She sings **really** well.

ACTIVITY 6 **Writing Adverbs of Degree in Two Sentences**

Write each pair of sentences. Use the adverb of degree in the correct place. Use correct capital letters, commas, and periods.

1. (very) i like bananas they are delicious

   I like bananas. They are very delicious.

2. (really) i like this chocolate cake a lot it is good

3. (very) the math test was difficult matt did not pass it

4. (too) jenna wants to play tennis today but it is hot maybe she will play tomorrow

5. (very) the problems in our country are serious no one can fix them

6. (extremely) everyone should vote it is an important thing to do

Common Student Mistakes

Student Mistake X	Problem	Correct Example ✓
In the early summer of **2010 my** father got a new job in London.	comma missing after adverb of time that begins a sentence	In the early summer of 2010**,** my father got a new job in London.
She speaks **well** English and French.	placement of adverb of manner	She speaks **English and French well.**
I do **always** my homework.	placement of adverb of frequency	I **always do** my homework.
This cheese is **too** delicious.	use of **too** with a positive word	This cheese is **really** delicious.

ACTIVITY 7 Scrambled Sentences

Change the order of the words to write a correct sentence. Be careful with spelling, capital letters, final punctuation, and word order. If there is a comma, it must stay with its word as shown. Do not add any commas.

The Sapporo Snow Festival

1. hokkaido is sapporo a large island is the capital in northern japan, and

    _____

2. hokkaido in the summer many japanese tourists visit because is not so hot the weather

    _____

3. because people visit see the snow and ice they want to hokkaido in the winter

    _____

4. they usually come a lot of the to sapporo snow in early february festival snow when there is

    _____

5. hokkaido has winters because it is far north, so very long

    _____

6. it is really cold when the weather is cold,

_____

7. is −8 °C in january, the temperature around

_____

8. buildings with the build huge snow and people animals and ice

_____

9. are beautiful these and buildings animals very

_____

10. the sapporo is one of in the world snow festival the events most famous

_____

ACTIVITY 8 **Finding and Correcting 10 Mistakes**

Circle the ten mistakes. Then write the sentences correctly. The number in parentheses ( ) is the number of mistakes in that sentence. Be ready to explain your answers.

Saudi Arabia

Studying English in Three Countries

1. Fatima is from the Saudi Arabia, and she speaks English very well. (1)

_____

2. She takes three years of English in high school, and now she takes English classes at very good university. (2)

_____

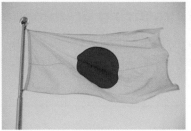

The Netherlands   Japan

3. Lucas and Thomas is from the Netherlands, and we speak English well. (2)

_____

4. Students in the Netherlands study English for very long time, so many of them speak English extremely well. (1)

_____

5. Kyoko is from Japan, and she is wants to improve his English conversation ability. (2)

_____

6. Students in Japan did not have many chances to use their English but many schools want to change this situation. (2)

_____

Track 7 •))   **ACTIVITY 9**   **Dictation**

You will hear six sentences three times. Listen carefully and write the six sentences. The number in parentheses ( ) is the number of words in the sentence. Be careful with capital letters and end punctuation.

1. _____ (8)

2. _____ (6)

3. _____ (7)

4. _____ (10)

5. _____ (8)

6. _____ (12)

ACTIVITY 10 **Practicing Grammar and Vocabulary in Model Writing**

Read the sentences in the paragraph very carefully. Fill in the missing words from the word bank. Circle the 11 letters that need to be capital letters. Add commas in the correct places. Then copy the paragraph on your own paper.

supermarket	about	but	sometimes	from his house
every day	about	really	because	carefully

My Neighbor

1 this is a story _____ my neighbor. **2** his name is mr taylor.

3 he is _____ 80 years old but he drives his car _____.

4 he is old so he drives very _____. **5** _____ he drives very slowly many other cars pass by him. **6** he drives from his house to the _____ twice a week.

7 _____ he drives _____ to the bank. **8** mr taylor drives well _____ i am _____ afraid when i see him in his car.

Write the paragraph from Activity 10 again, but make the changes listed below and all other necessary changes.

<u>Sentence 2</u>. Change **Mr. Taylor** to a different name. (Look at the photo below for ideas.)

<u>Sentence 3</u>. Change **80** to **18**. Change **but** to **and**.

<u>Sentence 4</u>. Change the adjective to make it match the photo below. Make the second verb negative.

<u>Sentence 5</u>. Change **slowly** to its opposite. Add the word **can't** to the second verb.

<u>Sentences 6 and 7</u>. In these two sentences, change the places after the preposition **to**. Choose places that match the person in the photo below.

<u>Sentence 8</u>. Change the name to match sentence 2. Make the first verb negative. Change the word **but** to **so.**

_____

_____

_____

_____

_____

_____

_____

Building Vocabulary and Spelling

Learning Words with the Sound of ow in flower*

ow = f l **o** **w** e r   This sound is usually spelled with the letters **ou** and **ow**.

flower

house

ACTIVITY 12 **Which Words Do You Know?**

This list has 35 common words with the sound of <u>ow</u> in fl<u>ow</u>er.

1. Notice the spelling patterns.

2. Check ✓ the words you know.

3. Look up new words in a dictionary. Write the meanings in your Vocabulary Notebook.

Common Words

GROUP 1:
Words spelled with **ou**

☐ 1. a b **ou** t

☐ 2. a r **ou** n d

☐ 3. c l **ou** d

☐ 4. c **ou** n t

☐ 5. f l **ou** r

☐ 6. f **ou** n d

☐ 7. g r **ou** n d

☐ 8. h **ou** r

☐ 9. h **ou** s e

☐ 10. l **ou** d

☐ 11. m **ou** s e

☐ 12. m **ou** n t a i n

☐ 13. m **ou** t h

☐ 14. **ou** r

☐ 15. **ou** t

☐ 16. p **ou** n d

☐ 17. r **ou** n d

☐ 18. s h **ou** t

☐ 19. s **ou** n d

☐ 20. s **ou** r

☐ 21. s **ou** t h

*List is from: Spelling Vocabulary List © 2013 Keith Folse

GROUP 2:

Words spelled with **ow**

☐ 22. a l l **o w**

☐ 23. b **o w**

☐ 24. b r **o w** n

☐ 25. c **o w**

☐ 26. c r **o w** d e d

☐ 27. d **o w** n

☐ 28. f l **o w** e r

☐ 29. h **o w**

☐ 30. n **o w**

☐ 31. p **o w** e r

☐ 32. s h **o w** e r

☐ 33. t **o w** el

☐ 34. t **o w** n

☐ 35. v **o w** e l

ACTIVITY 13 Matching Words and Pictures

Use the list in Activity 12 to write the common word that matches the picture.

1. _____

4. _____

7. _____

2. _____

5. _____

8. _____

3. _____

6. _____

ACTIVITY 18 **Spelling Review: Which Word Is Correct?**

This review covers the different ways of spelling **ow** in fl**ow**er in this unit. Read each pair of words. Circle the word that is spelled correctly.

	A	B			A	B
1.	house	howse		**11.**	sour	sowr
2.	pound	pownd		**12.**	allou	allow
3.	our	owr		**13.**	found	fownd
4.	doun	down		**14.**	south	sowth
5.	mouth	mowth		**15.**	pouer	power
6.	mouse	mowse		**16.**	touel	towel
7.	cou	cow		**17.**	hou	how
8.	about	abowt		**18.**	shout	showt
9.	shour	shower		**19.**	crouded	crowded
10.	hour	howr		**20.**	cloud	clowd

ACTIVITY 19 **Spelling Review**

Read the four words in each row. Underline the word that is spelled correctly.

	A	B	C	D
1.	flowr	floore	flouwer	flower
2.	famows	famosu	famous	feimos
3.	kitchn	kitchin	kitchen	ketchen
4.	posible	bosibul	possible	bossible
5.	countain	counten	contain	conten
6.	shold	should	shuld	showld
7.	femli	femili	famly	family
8.	papper	pepper	peapper	pipper
9.	minits	minutes	menutes	menits
10.	studente	estudent	student	stdent

A	B	C	D
11. money	mony	mouney	moni
12. haous	hows	house	hause
13. taol	taowel	touwel	towel
14. bcause	bcose	becose	because
15. clothes	clotese	clouthes	clouethes
16. finaly	finally	finali	finalli
17. soas	saus	sauce	sose
18. reason	renson	raisone	rason
19. arounde	arownde	arownd	around
20. evribody	evribady	everybady	everybody

Original Student Writing

Writing Your Ideas in Sentences or a Paragraph

Write eight to twelve sentences on your own paper. Write about a person you know. This person can be a friend, neighbor, or someone famous. Be sure to use adverbs of place, time, manner, frequency, and degree. For help, you can follow the examples in Activity 10 or Activity 11.

Peer Editing

Exchange papers from the above activity. Read your partner's sentences.
Then use Peer Editing Sheet 3 on ELTNGL.com/sites/els to make comments about the writing.

PREPARING TO READ

BUILDING
VOCABULARY

A Use the words in **blue** to complete the sentences.

> model   engineers   describe   drawings

1. Some _____ make bridges and buildings. Others make computers and cell phones.

2. Did you see his _____ of his cat? He used a pencil to make them.

3. I use two words to _____ my brother: tall and funny.

4. Look at that tiny _____ train. It looks just like a real train.

BUILDING
VOCABULARY

B Read the questions. Choose the correct answers.

1. Which **floats** in water?
   a. a coin   b. a plastic bottle

2. Which **sinks** in water?
   a. wood   b. a rock

3. Which is a **machine**?
   a. a dishwasher   b. a ball

4. Which did man **invent**?
   a. the car   b. trees

USING
VOCABULARY

C Respond to each of the prompts below.

1. Name a machine you use. _____

2. Describe the machine in two or three words. _____
   _____

3. Make a drawing of the machine on a separate piece of paper. Show it to a partner.

THE FATHER OF ENGINEERING 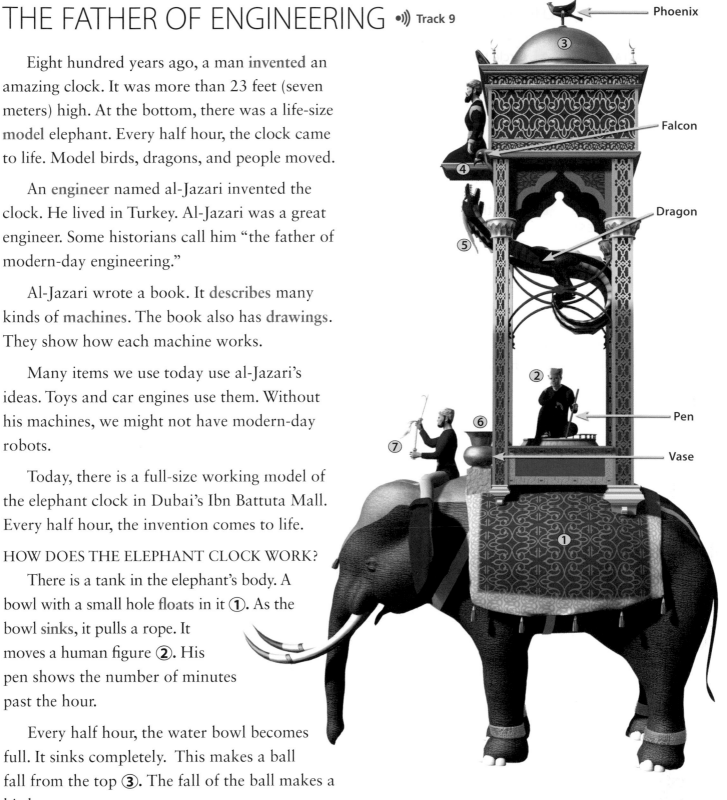 •))) Track 9

Eight hundred years ago, a man **invented** an amazing clock. It was more than 23 feet (seven meters) high. At the bottom, there was a life-size **model** elephant. Every half hour, the clock came to life. Model birds, dragons, and people moved.

An **engineer** named al-Jazari invented the clock. He lived in Turkey. Al-Jazari was a great engineer. Some historians call him "the father of modern-day engineering."

Al-Jazari wrote a book. It **describes** many kinds of **machines**. The book also has **drawings**. They show how each machine works.

Many items we use today use al-Jazari's ideas. Toys and car engines use them. Without his machines, we might not have modern-day robots.

Today, there is a full-size working model of the elephant clock in Dubai's Ibn Battuta Mall. Every half hour, the invention comes to life.

HOW DOES THE ELEPHANT CLOCK WORK?

There is a tank in the elephant's body. A bowl with a small hole **floats** in it ①. As the bowl **sinks**, it pulls a rope. It moves a human figure ②. His pen shows the number of minutes past the hour.

Every half hour, the water bowl becomes full. It sinks completely. This makes a ball fall from the top ③. The fall of the ball makes a bird move.

The ball then drops out of another bird's mouth. It falls into a dragon's mouth ④. The ball makes the dragon's head move ⑤, and the dragon's tail pulls the bowl back up.

Finally, the ball drops into a vase ⑥. This makes the elephant driver move ⑦. The cycle[1] begins again until there are no more balls at the top.

[1] A **cycle** is a series of events.

Phoenix

Falcon

Dragon

Pen

Vase

◄ **A painting of Ada Lovelace in Whitechapel Art Gallery, London**

THE MOTHER OF COMPUTING ◉)) Track 10

On October 16 every year, people **celebrate** Ada Lovelace Day. Who is Ada Lovelace?

You probably know the names Bill Gates and Steve Jobs. Men like them had a **huge** effect on the world of computers. But who created the first computer program? Many historians believe it was a woman: Lady Augusta Ada King. She also used the name Ada Lovelace.

Lovelace was born in 1815. She **grew up** in London, England. Her mother was a mathematician. As a child, Lovelace was **brilliant** at math and science.

At the age of 17, Lovelace met a mathematician. His name was Charles Babbage. They enjoyed **discussing** math. Babbage had a project. It was a machine called an "Analytical Engine." He wanted the machine to work on difficult math problems.

In 1843, Lovelace helped write an article on the machine. In the article, she described an idea. It was a step-by-step calculation for the machine. Today, people think of the Analytical Engine as the first design of a computer. And they think of Lovelace's step-by-step calculation as the first computer **program**.

There were very few female mathematicians and scientists back then. Today, many more women study math and science. But there are still fewer women studying these subjects. What is the **reason** Ada Lovelace Day is important? It celebrates women in science, engineering, and mathematics. Lovelace is an important role model for young women around the world.

UNDERSTANDING THE READING

A Circle the two main ideas of the text.

1. Lovelace had a huge effect on the world of computers.

2. Babbage's project was a machine called an "Analytical Engine."

3. Lovelace is an important role model for young women around the world.

4. Lovelace's step-by-step calculation is the first computer program.

B Read each statement. Circle *True* or *False*.

1. Ada Lovelace Day is on October 16.   True   False

2. Bill Gates created the first computer program.   True   False

3. Lovelace grew up in London.   True   False

4. Lovelace's father was a mathematician.   True   False

C Take a poll of your classmates: Who is interested in math and science? How many men? How many women? Use the poll to discuss the prompts with a partner.

1. I think many women <u>are / are not</u> interested in math and science today. I think this because _____.

2. I think Ada Lovelace Day <u>is / is not</u> important because _____
   _____.

PREPARING TO READ

BUILDING
VOCABULARY

A Use the words in **blue** to complete the sentences.

> reach   discovered   single

1. Earth has a _____ sun.

2. The mountain climber will soon _____ the top of the mountain.

3. In 2008, a one-year old child _____ a two-million-year-old bone in South Africa.

BUILDING
VOCABULARY

B Read the questions. Choose the correct answers.

1. Which word describes **stars**?
    a. bright   b. black

2. Which is a **planet**?
    a. China   b. Earth

3. Which is necessary for **life**?
    a. water   b. clothes

USING
VOCABULARY

C Read the questions. What do you think? Circle *Yes* or *No*.

1. Can technology help us find new planets?   Yes / No
2. Are there any other planets like Earth?   Yes / No
3. Is it possible that other planets have water?   Yes / No
4. Can we easily reach other planets today?   Yes / No

An artist's idea of the surface of an exoplanet in the Trappist-1 star system

In the future, a starship like this might carry thousands of people to a new home planet.

OTHER WORLDS •))) Track 11

Look up at the sky at night. There are thousands of **stars**. But are there other **planets** like Earth? And could humans live there one day?

Astronomers are using new technology. They are **discovering** hundreds of new planets. There are at least 3,500 "exoplanets" so far. Exoplanets are planets that move around stars other than the sun. Some exoplanets may be similar to Earth.

What makes an exoplanet Earthlike? It needs to be far enough from its star. This gives it the right temperature for living things. It also means it might have water. With water, there might also be **life**.

In 2016, scientists found seven Earthlike exoplanets around a **single** star—Trappist-1.

Each planet is Earthlike in size. Each may have water. The planets are very close to the star. But it is much cooler than our sun. So there could be life on the planets.

Could humans live on an Earthlike planet one day? The biggest problem is distance. In 2016, scientists found an Earthlike exoplanet about 4.3 lightyears from Earth. But with today's technology, we will need thousands of years to get there.

This may change with future technology. Andreas Tziolas is a scientist. He thinks we might travel to another solar system one day. He believes new technology will make many things possible. He believes we will **reach** the nearest star in a few decades, and travel between stars within a hundred years.

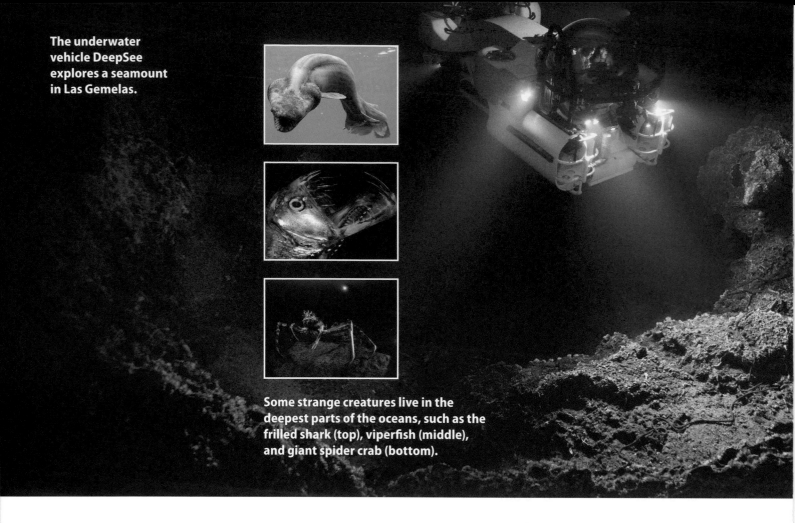

The underwater vehicle DeepSee explores a seamount in Las Gemelas.

Some strange creatures live in the deepest parts of the oceans, such as the frilled shark (top), viperfish (middle), and giant spider crab (bottom).

HIDDEN DEPTHS ■))) Track 12

Oceans are a mystery. In the past, people believed there were monsters in the seas. Others imagined mermaids and underwater cities.

Today, much of the ocean is still a mystery. Dr. Robert Ballard is an oceanography professor. He says, "The oceans cover 71 percent of our planet. Yet only 5 percent of it has been explored."

MOUNTAINS IN THE SEA

New technology is helping scientists explore these hidden worlds. For example, scientists are using an underwater vehicle called DeepSee. They used it to study Las Gemelas. This is an area of underwater mountains near Costa Rica. A huge variety of species lives there. Some of these species are new to the scientists. Some

may have important chemicals. These chemicals can help people fight illnesses, such as cancer.

DOWN IN THE DEPTHS

The deepest place on Earth is the Mariana Trench. It is in the Pacific Ocean. The ocean floor there is about 36,000 feet (11,000 meters) deep. In 2012, filmmaker and explorer James Cameron reached the Mariana Trench. He used a vehicle called Deepsea Challenger. Cameron took photos and collected underwater samples.

Technology is helping us discover new animals and plants. Some are millions of years old. These discoveries can help us better understand how life on our planet began. As Cameron says, "This is the beginning of opening up [a] new frontier."

UNDERSTANDING THE READING

A Circle the gist of the text.

UNDERSTANDING THE GIST

1. Today, much of the ocean is a mystery.

2. Some sea and plant animals are millions of years old.

3. New technology is helping scientists explore the ocean.

4. Scientists are using an underwater vehicle called DeepSee.

B Choose the correct answers to complete the sentences.

UNDERSTANDING DETAILS

1. The oceans cover _____ percent of our planet
   a. 7   b. 71   c. 50

2. Scientists used DeepSee to explore _____.
   a. Las Gemelas   b. Costa Rica   c. the Mariana Trench

3. The Mariana Trench is about _____ feet deep.
   a. 36,000   b. 3,000   c. 63,000

4. Scientists are discovering new _____ in the ocean
   a. rocks and shells   b. animals and plants   c. sand and seaweed

C Imagine you could speak with James Cameron about the Mariana Trench. Write some questions to ask about the sea. Use any of the sentence starters below. Then work with a partner to role-play an interview with Cameron.

EXPANDING UNDERSTANDING

Was the Mariana Trench _____?

Did you see _____?

Did you take _____?

How did you _____?

Why did you _____?

Do you want to _____?

GRAMMAR REFERENCE

UNIT 1
Language for Writing: Simple Past Tense of *Be* and Other Verbs

Be			Other verbs		
I He She It	**was**	happy. sad. here. at work.	I You We They He She It		**play<u>ed</u>** soccer. **went** to the store. **had** lunch.
	was not (wasn't)				
You We They	**were**			**didn't**	**have** lunch **play** soccer. **go** to the store.
	were not (weren't)				

UNIT 3
Language for Writing: Modal Verbs for Predictions

Affirmative			Negative		
I You We They He She It	**will ('ll)** **might** **may**	**be** late. **arrive** soon.	I You We They He She It	**will not (won't)** **might not** **may not**	**be** on time. **arrive** until later.

Note: Use *will* for things that are certain. Use *might* or *may* for things that are uncertain.

EDITING CHECKLIST

Use the checklist to find errors in your writing task for each unit.

	WRITING TASK	
	1	2
1. Is the first word of every sentence capitalized?		
2. Does every sentence end with the correct punctuation?		
3. Does every sentence contain a subject and a verb?		
4. Do your subjects and verbs agree?		
5. Do all possessive nouns have an apostrophe?		
6. Are all proper nouns capitalized?		
7. Is the spelling of places, people, and other proper nouns correct?		

Read each paragraph and answer the questions that follow.

Example Paragraph 1

The Best Place to Relax

My back **porch** is my favorite place to **relax**. First, it has lots of comfortable chairs with soft pillows. I feel so good when I sit in them. My back porch is also very peaceful. I can sit and think there. I can even read a great book and nobody **bothers** me. Finally, in the evening, I can sit on my porch and watch the sunset. Watching the beautiful colors always calms me. I can relax in many places, but my back porch is the best.

a porch: a part at the front or back of a house with only a floor and a roof

to relax: to rest or do something enjoyable

to bother: to make someone feel worried or upset

Post-Reading

1. How many sentences are in this paragraph? _____

2. What is the main topic of this paragraph? (Circle.)

    a. The writer likes watching the sunset.

    b. The writer likes to read a book in a quiet place.

    c. The writer likes to relax on her back porch.

3. What is the first sentence of this paragraph? (This is the topic sentence.) Write it here.

    _____

    _____

4. The writer gives examples of how her porch is relaxing. List the four things the writer does to relax on her porch.

    a. ___The writer sits in comfortable chairs._____

    b. _____

    c. _____

    d. _____

5. Read the paragraph again. Find at least two adjectives and write them below.

    _____

6. Read the topic (first) sentence and the concluding (last) sentence of the paragraph. Write down the ideas that these two sentences have in common.

    _____

Example Paragraph 2

Taipei 101

    I work in one of the world's tallest buildings—Taipei 101. This building is in Taipei's business **district**. Taipei 101 opened to the public in 2004. It is made of **steel** and glass panels, so it has a beautiful silver color. It has 101 **floors**. There are even five more levels below the building! Many international businesses have offices in Taipei 101. There are great places to shop in the building, too. I am **proud** to work in such an important place.

a district: an area

steel: a very strong metal

a floor: a level of a building

proud: having a very happy feeling of satisfaction

Post-Reading

1. How many sentences are in this paragraph? _____

2. What is the main topic of this paragraph? (Circle.)

    a. information about a city

    b. information about a person

    c. information about a building

3. What is the first sentence of this paragraph? (This is the topic sentence.) Write it here.

    _____

    _____

4. Answer these questions in complete sentences.

    a. Where is the building?

    _____

    b. How old is the building?

    _____

    c. What color is the building?

    _____

    d. How many floors does the building have in total?

    _____

5. Read the paragraph again. Find at least four adjectives and write them below.

_____

6. Read the topic (first) sentence and the concluding (last) sentence of the paragraph. Write down the ideas that these two sentences have in common.

_____

Parts of a Paragraph: The Topic Sentence

Every good paragraph has a **topic sentence**. The topic sentence is one sentence that tells the main idea of the whole paragraph.

The topic sentence:

- is usually the first sentence in the paragraph
- should not be too specific or too general
- must describe the information in all the sentences of the paragraph

If a paragraph does not have a topic sentence, the reader may be confused because the ideas will not be organized clearly. Make sure every paragraph has a topic sentence!

ACTIVITY 2 Practicing Topic Sentences

Read each paragraph and the three topic sentences below it. Choose the best topic sentence and write it on the lines. Then read the paragraph again. Make sure that the topic sentence gives the main idea for the whole paragraph. Remember to indent.

Example Paragraph 3

Beautiful Snow?

_____

_____ Snow is beautiful when it falls. After a few days, the snow is not beautiful anymore. It starts to **melt**, and the clean streets become **messy**. It is difficult to walk anywhere. The **sidewalks** are **slippery**. Snow also causes traffic problems. Some roads are closed. Other roads are **hard** to drive on safely. Drivers have more **accidents** on snowy roads. I understand why some people like snow, but I do not like it very much.

    a. In December, it usually snows.

    b. Some people like snow, but I do not.

    c. I love snow.

to melt: to change from ice to liquid

messy: sloppy; dirty

a sidewalk: a paved walkway on the side of roads

slippery: causing a person to slip or slide, usually because of a smooth surface

hard: difficult

an accident: a car crash

Maria and Her Great Job

_____ She works at Papa Joe's Restaurant. She **serves** about 60 people every day. Maria can remember all the dinner orders. If there is a problem with any of the food, she **takes** it **back** to the kitchen **immediately.** Maria works very hard to make sure all her customers have a great meal.

to serve: to give someone food and drink at a restaurant

to take back: to return

immediately: at that moment; very quickly

    a. My cousin Maria is an excellent server.

    b. My cousin Maria works at Papa Joe's Restaurant.

    c. Maria's customers do not eat big meals.

My Favorite City

_____ I love to see all the interesting things there. The city is big, exciting, and full of life. I always visit the Statue of Liberty and the Empire State Building. I also visit Chinatown. At night, I go to **shows** on Broadway. The food in the city is excellent, too. I truly enjoy New York City.

a show: a live performance on stage

    a. I like to see the Statue of Liberty and the Empire State Building.

    b. New York is a very big city.

    c. My favorite city in the world is New York.

Parts of a Paragraph: The Concluding Sentence

In addition to a topic sentence and body, every good paragraph has a **concluding sentence**. The concluding sentence ends the paragraph with a final thought.

The concluding sentence:

- often gives a summary of the information in the paragraph
- often gives information that is similar to the information in the topic sentence
- can be a **suggestion**, **opinion**, or **prediction**
- should <u>not</u> give any new information about the topic

Choosing Concluding Sentences

Read each paragraph and the three concluding sentences below it. Choose the best concluding sentence and write it on the lines. Then read the paragraph again. Make sure that the concluding sentence gives a final thought for the whole paragraph.

Example Paragraph 6

Monday

I hate Monday for many reasons. One reason is work. I get up early to go to work on Monday. After a weekend of fun and relaxation, I do not like to do this. Another reason that I do not like Monday is that I have three meetings every Monday. These meetings last a long time, and they are **extremely** boring. Traffic is also a big problem on Monday. There are more cars on the road on Monday. Drivers are in a bad **mood**, and I must be more careful than usual. _____

_____

extremely: very

a mood: a person's emotion at a particular time

a. Monday is worse than Tuesday, but it is better than Sunday.

b. I do not like meetings on Monday.

c. These are just a few reasons why I do not like Monday.

Example Paragraph 7

Buying a Car

Buying a car **requires** careful planning. Do you want a new or a used car? This depends on how much money you can spend. Sometimes a used car needs repairs. What style of car do you want? You can look at many different models to help you decide. Next, do you want extra **features** in your new car? Adding lots of extra features makes a car more expensive. Finally, you have to decide where you will buy your car. _____

_____

to require: to need

a feature: an option, such as a DVD player or tinted windows

a. It is important to think about all of these things when you are buying a car.

b. The most important thing is the kind of car that you want to buy.

c. Will you buy your new car from a friend or a car dealer?

Hanami

Hanami is a very popular Japanese tradition. Every spring, thousands of **cherry** trees bloom all over Japan. For two weeks during Hanami, friends and families gather in parks and the countryside to see the beautiful flowers and celebrate the end of their vacation time. People make lots of food and have huge picnics under the lovely trees. There is lots of music and dancing, and large groups of people walk through the parks together. The celebration often continues into the night, and there are **lanterns** everywhere to light the celebration. _____

a cherry: a small red fruit

a lantern: a light with a decorative cover

a. People like to be with their family and friends during Hanami.

b. Looking at flowers during Hanami is interesting.

c. This is truly a most beloved Japanese custom.

Writing the English Alphabet

A a	B b	C c	D d	E e	F f	G g	H h	I i	J j
K k	L l	M m	N n	O o	P p	Q q	R r	S s	T t
U u	V v	W w	X x	Y y	Z z				

✓ Therez are 26 letters in the English alphabet.

   5 are vowels: A E I O U

   21 are consonants: B C D F G H J K L M N P Q R S T V W X Y Z

✓ When **w** and **y** come after a vowel, these two letters are silent vowels: **saw, grow, play, toy, buy.**

✓ When **w** and **y** are at the beginning of a syllable, they are consonant sounds: **wake, wish, when, year, young.**

Definitions of Useful Language Terms

Adjective An adjective is a word that describes a noun.

> Lexi is a very **smart** girl.

Adverb An adverb is a word that describes a verb, an adjective, or another adverb.

> The secretary types **quickly**. She types **very quickly**.

Article The definite article is *the*. The indefinite articles are *a* and *an*.

> **The** teacher gave **an** assignment to **the** students.
> Jillian is eating **a** banana.

Clause A clause is a group of words that has a subject-verb combination. Sentences can have one or more clauses.

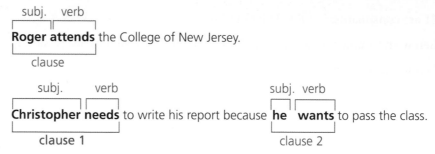

Noun A noun is a person, place, thing, or idea.

> **Sandra** likes to eat **sandwiches** for lunch.
> **Love** is a very strong **emotion**.

Object An object is a word that comes after a transitive verb or a preposition.

> Jim bought a new **car**.
> I left my **jacket** in the **house**.

Predicate A predicate is the part of a sentence that shows what a subject does.

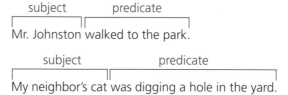

Preposition A preposition is a word that can show location, time, and direction. Some common prepositions are *around, at, behind, between, from, on, in, near, to, over, under,* and *with*. Prepositions can also consist of two words (*next to*) or three words (*in addition to*).

Punctuation Punctuation includes the period (.), comma (,), question mark (?), and exclamation point (!).

Subject The subject of a sentence tells who or what the sentence is about.

> **My science teacher** gave us a homework assignment. **It** was difficult.

Tense A verb has tense. Tense shows when the action happened.

Simple Present:	She **walks** to school every day.
Present Progressive:	She **is walking** to school now.
Simple Past:	She **walked** to school yesterday.
Past Progressive:	She **was walking** to school when she saw her friend.
Simple Future:	She **is going to walk** to school tomorrow.
Simple Future:	She **will walk** to school tomorrow.

Verb   A verb is a word that shows the action of a sentence.

They **speak** French.

My father **works** at the power plant.

Review of Verb Tenses

Verb Tense	Affirmative	Negative	Usage
Simple Present	I work you take he studies she does we play they have	I do not work you do not take he does not study she does not do we do not play they do not have	• for routines, habits, and other actions that happen regularly • for facts and general truths
Simple Past	I worked you took he studied she did we played they had	I did not work you did not take he did not study she did not do we did not play they did not have	• for actions that were completed in the past
Present Progressive	I am working you are taking he is studying she is doing we are playing they are having*	I am not working you are not taking he is not studying she is not doing we are not playing they are not having*	• for actions that are happening now • for future actions if a future time adverb is used or understood
Simple Future (*Be Going To*)	I am going to work you are going to take he is going to study she is going to do we are going to play they are going to have	I am not going to work you are not going to take he is not going to study she is not going to do we are not going to play they are not going to have	• for plans that are already made • for predictions based on an action happening in the present
Simple Future (*Will*)	I will work you will take he will study she will do we will play they will have	I will not work you will not take he will not study she will not do we will not play they will not have	• for future plans or decisions that are made at the moment of speaking • for strong predictions • for promises/offers to help
Present Perfect	I have worked you have taken he has studied she has done we have played they have had	I have not worked you have not taken he has not studied she has not done we have not played they have not had	• for actions that began in the past and continue until the present • for actions in the indefinite past time • for repeated actions in the past
Past Progressive	I was working you were taking he was studying she was doing we were playing they were having*	I was not working you were not taking he was not studying she was not doing we were not playing they were not having*	• for longer actions in the past that are interrupted by other actions or events

Have can be used in progressive tenses only when it has an active meaning in special expressions, such as:

- *have* a party
- *have* a good time
- *have* a bad time
- *have* a baby

Capitalization Rules

1. The first word in a sentence is capitalized.

    I go to the movies every week.

    Deserts are beautiful places to visit.

2. The pronoun *I* is always capitalized.

    Larry and **I** are brothers.

3. People's formal and professional titles begin with capital letters.

    Mr. and **M**rs. Jenkins are on vacation.

    Lisa saw **D**r. Johansen at the bank yesterday.

4. Proper names (specific people and places) begin with capital letters.

    The **C**oliseum in **R**ome is a beautiful old monument.

    Kate met her brother **A**lex at the park.

5. Names of streets begin with capital letters.

    Ruth lives on **W**ilson **A**venue.

6. Geographical locations (cities, states, countries, continents, lakes, and rivers) begin with capital letters.

    I am going to travel to **L**ondon, **E**ngland, next week.

    The **A**rno **R**iver passes through **T**uscany, **I**taly.

7. The names of languages and nationalities begin with capital letters.

    My grandmother speaks **P**olish.

    Jessica is going to learn **J**apanese.

    Melissa is **V**enezuelan, but her husband is **C**uban.

8. Most words in titles of paragraphs, essays, and books are capitalized. The first letter of a title is always capitalized, and the other important words in a title are capitalized. Do not capitalize prepositions (*to, in*), conjunctions (*and, but*), or articles (*a, an, the*) unless they are the first word of the title.

    *The **L**ife of **B**illy **B**arnes*

    *Crime and **P**unishment*

    *The **C**atcher in the **R**ye*

    *In the **B**edroom*

9. Specific course names are capitalized.

    Nick is taking **H**istory 101 at 10:00 A.M.

    Nick is taking history this semester. (general subject—no capital letter)

Eight Common Comma Rules

1. Put a comma before *and, but, for, or, nor, so,* and *yet* when they connect two simple sentences. This creates a compound sentence.

    Rick bought Julia a croissant**,** but he ate it himself.

2. Put a comma between three or more items in a list or series.

    Jen brought a towel**,** an umbrella**,** some sunscreen**,** and a book to the beach.

3. Put a comma after a dependent clause (a clause that begins with a connecting word) when that clause begins a sentence. This is called a complex sentence.

> Because it was raining outside, Alex used his umbrella.

4. Put a comma before or after the name of a person spoken to.

> "Hamad, do you want to play soccer?" Ana asked.
>
> "Do you want to play soccer, Hamad?" Ana asked.

5. Commas separate parts of dates and places. Put a comma between the day and the date. Put a comma between the date and the year. Put a comma between a city and a state or a country. Put an additional comma after the state or country name if it appears in the middle of a sentence.

> I was born on Tuesday, June 27, 1992.
>
> The concert was in Busan, Korea.
>
> The headquarters of that company is located in Osaka, Japan.
>
> I lived in Phuket, Thailand, for ten years.

6. Use a comma to separate an introductory word or phrase from the rest of the sentence.

> Finally, they decided to ask the police for help.
>
> Every afternoon after school, I go to the library.

NOTE: *Then* is not followed by a comma.

7. Use a comma to separate information that is not necessary in a sentence.

> Rome, which is the capital of Italy, has a lot of pollution.
>
> George Washington, the first president of the United States, was a military officer.

8. Put a comma after the salutation in personal letters and after the closing in personal and business letters.

Dear Roberta,	Dear Dr. Gomez,	Dear Ms. Kennedy,
With love,	Sincerely,	Yours truly,
Grandma	Jonathan	Alicia

Spelling Rules for Regular Simple Present Verbs and Plural Nouns

1. Add -*s* to the base form of most verbs and to most nouns.

run	runs
work	works
love	loves

2. If a verb/noun ends in an *x*, *z*, *s*, *sh*, or *ch*, add -*es*.

box	boxes
buzz	buzzes
pass	passes
push	pushes
watch	watches

3. If a verb/noun ends in a consonant + *y*, change the *y* to *i* and add -*es*.

carry	carries
worry	worries
party	parties

4. If a verb/noun ends in a vowel + *y*, add -*s*. Do not change the *y*.

pay	pays
boy	boys
destroy	destroys

5. Add -*es* to *go* and *do*.

go	goes
do	does

Spelling Rules for Regular Simple Past Tense Verbs

1. Add -*ed* to the base form of most verbs.

start	started
finish	finished
wash	washed

2. Add only -*d* when the base form ends in an *e*.

live	lived
care	cared
die	died

3. If a verb ends in a consonant + *y*, change the *y* to *i* and add -*ed*.

dry	dried
carry	carried
study	studied

4. If a verb ends in a vowel + *y*, do not change the *y*. Just add -*ed*.

play	played
stay	stayed
destroy	destroyed

5. If a verb has one syllable and ends in a consonant + vowel + consonant (CVC), double the final consonant and add -*ed*.

stop	sto**pp**ed
CVC	
rob	ro**bb**ed
CVC	

6. If a verb ends in a *w* or *x*, do not double the final consonant. Just add -*ed*.

sew	sewed
mix	mixed

7. If a verb that ends in CVC has two syllables and the <u>second</u> syllable is stressed, double the final consonant and add -*ed*.

ad mit′	admi**tt**ed
oc cur′	occu**rr**ed
per mit′	permi**tt**ed

8. If a verb that ends in CVC has two syllables and the <u>first</u> syllable is stressed, do *not* double the final consonant. Just add -*ed*.

hap′ pen	happe**n**ed
lis′ ten	liste**n**ed
o′ pen	ope**n**ed

Irregular Simple Past Tense Verbs

These are some of the more common irregular verbs in English.

Base Form	Simple Past
be (am/is/are)	was/were
become	became
begin	began
bite	bit
bleed	bled
blow	blew
break	broke
bring	brought
build	built
buy	bought
catch	caught
choose	chose
come	came
cost	cost
cut	cut
do	did
draw	drew
drink	drank
drive	drove
eat	ate
fall	fell
feel	felt
fight	fought
find	found
flee	fled
forget	forgot
get	got
give	gave
grow	grew
have	had
hear	heard
hide	hid
hit	hit
hold	held

Base Form	Simple Past
hurt	hurt
keep	kept
know	knew
leave	left
let	let
lose	lost
make	made
pay	paid
put	put
read	read
run	ran
say	said
see	saw
sell	sold
send	sent
set	set
sing	sang
sink	sank
sit	sat
sleep	slept
speak	spoke
spend	spent
stand	stood
steal	stole
swim	swam
take	took
teach	taught
tell	told
think	thought
throw	threw
understand	understood
wear	wore
win	won
write	wrote

The Preposition *At*

Location: Use *at* for specific locations.

> Angela works **at** the First National Bank.
>
> I always do my homework **at** my desk.
>
> Joel met Jillian **at** the corner of Polk Street and Florida Avenue.

Time: Use *at* for specific times.

> My grammar class meets **at** 9:00 A.M. every day.
>
> The lunch meeting begins **at** noon.
>
> Cate does not like to walk alone **at** night.

Direction: Use *at* for motion toward a goal.

> My brother threw a ball **at** me.
>
> The robber pointed his gun **at** the policewoman.

The Preposition *On*

Location: Use *on* when there is contact between two objects. We also use *on* with streets.

> The picture is **on** the wall.
>
> He put his books **on** the kitchen table.
>
> Erin lives **on** Bayshore Boulevard.

Time: Use *on* with specific days or dates.

> Our soccer game is **on** Saturday.
>
> Your dentist appointment is **on** October 14.
>
> I was born **on** June 22, 1988.

The Preposition *In*

Location: Use *in* when something is inside another thing.

> The books are **in** the big box.
>
> I left my jacket **in** your car.
>
> Barbara lives **in** Istanbul.

Time: Use *in* for a specific period of time, a specific year, or a future time.

> I am going to graduate from college **in** three years.
>
> My best friend got married **in** 2006.
>
> Mr. Johnson always drinks four cups of coffee **in** the morning.
>
> We will meet you **in** ten minutes.

More Prepositions

Here are a few more common prepositions of location. Remember that a preposition is usually followed by a noun (or pronoun). In the chart, the preposition shows the location of the ball (in relation to the box).

Preposition	Example
in	The gift is **in** the box.
on	Marta's gift is **on** the table.
under	Pedro keeps his shoes **under** his bed.
above/over	Sheila held the umbrella **over** her head to stay dry.
between	The milk is **between** the eggs and the butter.
in front of	Mark was standing in **front of** the restaurant.
in back of/behind	My shirt fell **behind** my dresser.
across...from	There is a supermarket **across** the street **from** my house.
next to/beside	The mailman left the package **next to** the door.

Useful Connectors for Writing

Coordinating Conjunctions

Coordinating conjunctions are used to connect two independent clauses (sentences).

Note: A comma usually appears before a coordinating conjunction that separates two independent clauses. (An exception is when the two clauses are both very short.)

Purpose	Coordinating Conjunction	Example
To show reason	for*	He ate a sandwich, **for** he was hungry.
To add information	and	Carla lives in Toronto, **and** she is a student.
To add negative information	nor**	Roberto does not like opera, **nor** does he enjoy hip-hop.
To show contrast	but†	The exam was difficult, **but** everyone passed.
To give a choice	or	We can eat Chinese food, **or** we can order a pizza.
To show concession/contrast	yet†	The exam was difficult, **yet** everyone passed.
To show result	so	It was raining, **so** we decided to stay home last night.

*The conjunction **for** is not common in English. It may be used in literary writing, but it is almost never used in spoken English.

Notice that question word order is used in the clause that follows **nor.

†The conjunctions **but** and **yet** have similar meanings. However, **yet** is generally used to show a stronger contrast.

Many writers remember these conjunctions with the acronym **FANBOYS**. Each letter represents one conjunction: **F = for**, **A = and**, **N = nor**, **B = but**, **O = or**, **Y = yet**, and **S = so**.

Subordinating Conjunctions

Subordinating conjunctions are used to connect a dependent clause and an independent clause.

NOTE: When the sentence begins with the dependent clause, a comma should be used after that clause.

Purpose	Subordinating Conjunction	Example
To show reason/cause	because	He ate a sandwich **because** he was hungry.
	since	**Since** he was hungry, he ate a sandwich.
	as	**As** he was hungry, he ate a sandwich.
To show contrast	although	**Although** the exam was difficult, everyone passed.
	even though	**Even though** the exam was difficult, everyone passed.
	though	**Though** the exam was difficult, everyone passed.
	while	Deborah is a dentist **while** John is a doctor.
To show time relationship	after	**After** we ate dinner, we went to a movie.
	before	We ate dinner **before** we went to a movie.
	until	I will not call you **until** I finish studying.
	while	**While** the pasta is cooking, I will cut the vegetables.
	as	**As** I was leaving the office, it started to rain.
To show condition	if	**If** it rains tomorrow, we will stay home.
	even if	We will go to the park **even if** it rains tomorrow.

Useful Vocabulary for Better Writing

Try these useful words and phrases as you write your sentences and paragraphs. They can make your writing sound more academic, natural, and fluent.

Topic Sentences

Words and phrases	Examples
There are QUANTIFIER (ADJECTIVE) SUBJECT…	*There are* many good places to visit in my country.
SUBJECT *must follow* QUANTIFIER (ADJECTIVE) *steps to* VERB…	A tourist *must follow* several simple *steps to* get a visa to visit my country.
There are QUANTIFIER (ADJECTIVE) *types / methods / ways*…	*There are* three different *types* of runners.
It is ADJECTIVE *to* VERB…	*It is* easy *to* make ceviche.

Supporting Sentence Markers

Words and phrases	Examples
One NOUN…	*One* reason to visit my country is the wonderful weather.
Another NOUN… … *another* NOUN	*Another* reason to visit my country is the delicious food. The delicious food is *another* reason to visit my country.
The first / second / next / final NOUN…	*The final* reason to visit my country is its wonderful people.

Giving and Adding Examples

Words and phrases	Examples
For example, S + V. *For instance,* S + V.	My instructor gives us so much homework. *For example*, yesterday he gave us five pages of grammar work.

Concluding Sentences

Words and phrases	Examples
In conclusion, S + V.	*In conclusion,* I believe that my parents are the best in the world.
It is clear that S + V.	*It is clear that* Guatemala is the best tourist destination in South America.
If you follow these important steps in VERB + *-ING*…, S + V.	*If you follow these important steps in* fixing a computer, you will not need to call an expert.

Telling a Story

Words and phrases	Examples
When I was X, I would VERB…	When I was a teenager, I would go to the beach with my friends every day.
When I think about that time, S + V.	When I think about that time, I remember my grandparents' love for me.
I will never forget NOUN…	I will never forget the day I left my country.
I can still remember NOUN… I will always remember NOUN…	I can still remember the day I started my first job.
X was the best / worst day of my life.	My sixteenth birthday was the best day of my life.
Every time S +V, S + V.	Every time I tried to speak English, my tongue refused to work!

Describing a Process

Words and phrases	Examples
First (Second, Third, etc.), Next, … / After that, … / Then … Finally, …	First, you cut the fish and vegetables into small pieces. Next, you add the lime juice. After that, you add in the seasonings. Finally, you mix everything together well.
The first thing you should do is VERB…	The first thing you should do is wash your hands.
Before S + V, S + V.	Before you cut up the vegetables, you need to wash them.
After / When S + V, S + V. After that, S + V.	After you cut up the vegetables, you need to add them to the salad. After that, you need to mix the ingredients.
The last / final step is… Finally, …	The last step is adding your favorite salad dressing. Finally, you should add your favorite salad dressing.

Showing Cause and Effect

Words and phrases	Examples
Because S+ V, S + V. S + V because S + V. Because of NOUN, S + V. S + V because of NOUN.	Because I broke my leg, I could not move. I could not move because I broke my leg. Because of my broken leg, I could not move. I could not move because of my broken leg.
CAUSE, so RESULT.	My sister did not know what to do, so she asked my mother for advice.

Describing

Words and phrases	Examples
Prepositions of location: above, across, around, in, near, under…	The children raced their bikes around the school.
Descriptive adjectives: wonderful, delightful, dangerous, informative, rusty…	The bent, rusty bike squeaked when I rode it.
SUBJECT + BE + ADJECTIVE.	The Terra Cotta Warriors of Xian are amazing.
SUBJECT + BE + the most ADJECTIVE + NOUN.	To me, Thailand is the most interesting country in the world.
SUBJECT tastes / looks / smells / feels like NOUN.	My ID card looks like a credit card.

| SUBJECT + *BE* + *known* / *famous for its* NOUN. | France *is famous for its* cheese. |
| Adverbs of manner: *quickly, slowly, quietly, happily…* | I *quickly* wrote his phone number on a scrap of paper that I found on the table. |

Stating an Opinion

Words and phrases	Examples
Personally, I believe / think / feel / agree / disagree / suppose (*that*) S + V.	*Personally, I believe that* New York City should ban large sugary drinks.
VERB + *-ING should not be allowed.*	*Smoking* in public *should not be allowed.*
In my opinion / view / experience, S + V.	*In my opinion,* smoking is rude.
For this reason, S + V. *That is why I think that* S + V.	*That is why I think that* smoking should not be allowed in restaurants.
There are many benefits / advantages to VERB + *-ING.*	*There are many benefits to* swimming every day.
There are many drawbacks / disadvantages to VERB + *-ING.*	*There are many drawbacks to* eating most of your meals at a restaurant.
I prefer X [NOUN] *to* Y [NOUN].	*I prefer* soccer *to* football.
To me, VERB + *-ING makes* (*perfect*) *sense.*	*To me,* exercising every day *makes perfect sense.*
For all of these important reasons, I think / believe (*that*) S + V.	*For all of these important reasons, I think* smoking is bad for your health.

Arguing and Persuading

Words and phrases	Examples
It is important to remember that S+V.	*It is important to remember that* students only wear their uniforms during school hours.
According to a recent survey / poll, S + V.	*According to a recent poll,* 85 percent of high school students felt they had too much homework.
Even more important, S + V.	*Even more important,* statistics show the positive effects of school uniforms on student behavior.
SUBJECT *must / should / ought to* VERB.	Researchers *must* stop unethical animal testing.
I agree that S + V. *However,* S + V.	*I agree that* eating healthily is important. *However,* the government should not make food choices for us.

Reacting/Responding

Words and phrases	Examples
TITLE *by* AUTHOR *is a / an* (ADJECTIVE) NOUN.	*Harry Potter and the Goblet of Fire by* J.K. Rowling *is an* entertaining book to read.
My first reaction to the prompt / news / article / question was / is NOUN.	*My first reaction to the article was* anger.
When I read / looked at / thought about NOUN, *I was amazed / shocked / surprised…*	*When I read* the article, *I was surprised* to learn of his athletic ability.

NOTES

NOTES

NOTES

NOTES

NOTES